THESIS ON
CYBERJAYA

THESIS ON CYBERJAYA

HEGEMONY AND UTOPIANISM IN A SOUTHEAST ASIAN STATE

AZLY RAHMAN

authorHOUSE®

AuthorHouse™
1663 Liberty Drive
Bloomington, IN 47403
www.authorhouse.com
Phone: 1-800-839-8640

Published by AuthorHouse   11/17/2012

ISBN: 978-1-4685-4898-3 (sc)
ISBN: 978-1-4685-4897-6 (e)

Library of Congress Control Number: 2012903088

Table of Contents

List of Figures

List of Tables

PART 1

BACKGROUND

Chapter I

INTRODUCTION

"Everything is good as it leaves the hands of the Author of things; everything degenerates in the hands of man."

—From Book 1 of *Emile or On education* (Rousseau, 1979, p. 37).

This dissertation concerns how what is connotated by the phrase "digital or cybernetic revolution" is "inscribed" onto the landscape of humanity, particularly that of Malaysia, a state governed by what de Certeau (1984) might term as, the "scriptural economy."[1] It starts with the premise that a concept can become ideology, and then architectural landscape, and then a paradigm of control

---

[1]   For an elaborate discussion of de Certeau's lamentation on the passing of the oral tradition to the emergence of the literacy of technology ('cybernetic'), see Part IV of de Certeau, M. (1984). *The practice of everyday life* (S. Rendall, Trans.). (London: University of California Press.)

over political, cultural, and economic spaces.[2] It hopes to suggest how human beings are conditioned and opiated by signs and symbols produced and reproduced by those who own the means of technological and intellectual productions (Marx & Engels, 1967). The central feature of this dissertation is an exploration of the nature of hegemony as consciousness-production and the creation of what Varenne (2003) might term as "constraints of culture" rather than the creation of its "possibilities" for human liberation. I am exploring how ideas flow transculturally, become inscription, get installed as systems of control, and evolve into ideology that becomes yet another indigenized systems of thought and material—formation.

In my exploration of the concept of hegemony, I am concerned with its nature and the subdivisions it produces, as well as with how the system of consciousness-formation is layered in all its complexities and become what Marx would now perhaps call "prozac" of a higher potency and dosage. To this end, this study looks at the conceptualization and the building of the "intelligent" and "digital" city of Cyberjaya in hyper-modernizing Malaysia, a business capital and the economic nerve of a grand-scale real estate project called "Multimedia Super

---

[2]   An interesting illustration of how ideology becomes landscape in the context of the entertainment industry can be found in Kargon, R. H., & Molella, A. P. (2000). Culture, technology and constructed memory in Disney's new town: Techno-nostalgia in historical perspective. In M. R. Levin (Ed.), *Cultures of control*. (Amsterdam: Harwood Academic Publishers.)

Corridor" (henceforth, "MSC") of the regime of Mahathir Mohamad, her fourth Prime Minister.[3]

I propose that the introduction of new technologies into social spheres will facilitate the maintenance of ideology, which will then help direct policies, establish new institutions that will then create newer forms of hegemonic conditions that will continue to benefit the ruling class. I argue, hegemonic conditions, processes, and consequences will further advance the development of higher forms of technologies that will then, through the idea of human-machine interaction, establish better systems of control. Such a cyclical and structurally systematic operation, as I have suggested in the cycle of hegemony in Figure 1 below, determines the nature of the sophistication of hegemony. Hence, the owners of the means of production of technologies will also be executive directors of the processes.

---

[3]   At the time this dissertation is written, Mahathir Mohamad has governed Malaysia since 1981, and relinquished power on October 31, 2003. Along with Singapore's Lee Kuan Yew, Indonesia's Mohamed Suharto, and Philippines' Ferdinand Marcos, Mahathir represents the breed of South East Asian leaders who believe that leaders should stay in power for "as long as the people need them."

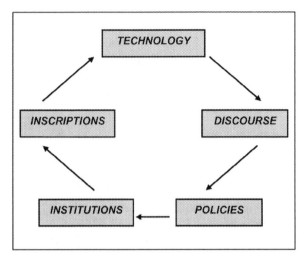

Figure 1: The Cycle of Hegemony

Rather than addressing hegemony merely from a "Gramscian" perspective, I choose to analyze this concept using a mixed-method approach. I call this formulation "towards a theory of hegemonic formations" and use multidimensional perspectives to look at how the concept of "cybernetics" transforms the development of this state in Southeast Asia. I hope to generate a "thick description" of the hegemonic process. This study looks at the "high and low stakes" of nations undergoing development in the age of high-speed globalization and ideological rapidization.

The idea of Malaysia's Multimedia Super Corridor (MSC), a grand project of social transformation, is a major feature of its political leadership's agenda for national development. University lecturers like me have been part of the class of "knowledge workers" mandated to explain to the people what these changes are about and how these benefit the *rakyat* ("the people"). I was a lecturer in Malaysia's sixth public university, Universiti

Utara Malaysia in Sintok, Kedah (which specializes in Management studies) teaching courses such as English as a Second Language, Foreign Policy, Management Ethics, and Thinking Skills. The mid-1990s saw the intensification of the development of Malaysia's management sciences based upon advanced principles of Taylorism (Schmidt & Finnigan, 1993; Vavrek, 1992) which then permeated into virtually all spheres of management, including perhaps "Islamic Management System." The idea of the MSC was part of the ethos of Information Systems Management, which would then be a formula to "cybernate" the nation towards progress and to "quantum leap" Malaysia into the Information Age (Mohamad, 1998). It was felt that the nation needed a newer set of installation as "commanding heights" of the scriptural economy. Mahathir Mohamad, the fourth prime minister oversaw the major national transformation. The ideology of technological progress and the notion of riding the waves of globalization along with the steering of the nation to a "Vision 2020" (a metaphorical date of the end of the benchmark of national development)—all these became the *raison d'etre* and the *leitmotif* of the Mahathir[4] regime.

---

[4]   The first name of Malaysia's fourth Prime Minister is used because that is what he is known as in Malaysia and throughout the world. In Malaysia, this is a normal convention of addressing someone even in a formal setting, i.e. Mr. + first name. In the case of Mahathir Mohamad, since he is a doctor by training, he is known as Dr. Mahathir.

Research Questions

My interest in this research is to find out how variant the concept of hegemony might be, beyond oftentimes what many a student of Gramsian Theory of Hegemony" might conceptualize. My questions are: If we are to speak of hegemony, what might be its subdivisions? What will be its transcultural dimensions? If we are to explain a nation's utopian ideals, as this study is also about, what are its properties?

Rationale for the Study

Why study Malaysia? It is an interesting state which can be looked at as a "laboratory of social and global experimentation" after having undergone historical periodizations such as pre-colonial kingdomship and "overlordships," colonialism, independence, development of statehood, and finally, participation in the globalized economy. The rationale of this study lies in investigating the role technology plays in the deep-structuring of hegemony and how it interplays with the political and the productive forces of the state. Another rationale lies in studying the way capitalism is characterized into what many scholars have termed as "informational" capitalism (Castells, 2000). I also hope to uncover the political psychology of control (see Marcuse, 1985) as the system has evolved culturally; a blend of traditional systems of control aided by an emergent system technologically-inspired (see Beniger, 1986). Below I further highlight the rationale for this study. They are:

1. In the field of international and transcultural studies, it is necessary to look at social changes at the level of world-systems. I am taking a multidisciplinary perspective in looking at the complexity of the phenomena of change.

2. In studying "hegemony" and how "systems of hegemony" operate, it is necessary to look at the concept from a transcultural perspective.

3. In studying how nations such as Malaysia "develop" along the path of "Western-led developmentalism," it is necessary to relate the issue of technological control to the question of "national sovereignty" especially when the world's economic system is characterized by "globalization."

4. In studying how nations like Malaysia undergo transitions and transformation, it is necessary to look at the dialectical process she undergoes, i.e. what are the contradictions inherent in the way the developmental project yields.

5. In studying how Malaysia, a nation in Southeast Asia, undergoes varied experiences in her national development project, it is necessary to analyze the nature of authority and the style of authoritarianism in the way the political system behaves. In this sense, we can discern the nature of change, continuity, and stability of the nation as it is dictated by the strong state and authoritarian regime.

Significance of the Study

Below, I highlight the significance of this study, or how this inquiry might contribute to the body of literature on the study of developing nations:

1. In studying the transcultural flow of ideas from the advanced West as they continue to be inscribed into national and sovereign system, this study on Cyberjaya will attempt to contribute to the field of development especially in the description of the fundamental character of a "new style of imperialism" as it operates in collaboration (or in "smart partnership") with the host regime.

2. In the field of international education development, this study will attempt to contribute to the understanding of the pattern of "hegemonic formation"—in the way the concept of "cybernetics" becomes enculturalized and becomes diffused in the public and local discourses.

3. In studying how a particular government, i. e. Malaysian, addresses the issue of globalization, I will highlight how the leaders of that government use a variety of devices to mediate the contradiction between "national free will" and "global corporate domination." Another contribution this study attempts to make is in the area of understanding how political actors address the issue of the "withering of the state."

4. In studying how language mirrors and alters reality, I draw examples from the transcultural flow of the word "cyber" as it passes through the cultural spheres of the host nation and becomes the

ideology and the consciousness of the people. The study will attempt to contribute to the burgeoning literature on discourse theory especially as it is applied to the study of developing nations.

5. In studying the idea of "inscriptions," a key feature of this dissertation, the study will attempt to contribute to our understanding of how "concepts get inscribed" onto the landscape and then become ideology which then become consciousness which ultimately continue to change the relations of production and brings about the creation of a technological culture.

The points above hence are some of the areas of significance of the study on the nature of changes a nation undergoes as a result of its conscious application of technology.

Organization of Chapters

There are four parts to this dissertation namely, 1) Background (consisting of Chapters I, II, and III); 2) History, Power, and Ideology (consisting of Chapters IV, V, and VI), 3) Inscription of Ideology (consisting of Chapters VII, VIII, IX, and X); and 4) Discussion (consisting of Chapters XI, XII, and XIII).

Part 1. Background.

In Chapter I; "Introduction," I provide the description, rationale, and significance of the study.

In Chapter II; "Review of Selected Literature," on the review of selected literature, I discuss the dominant idea of "cybernetics" and "information technology and how this concept has emerged to be the socio-psychological *leitmotif* and construct which has permeated the consciousness of humanity since the beginning of the second half of the last century. I also discuss the major concepts that underpin this study. They are "hegemony," "utopianism," "technological determinism," "globalization, "and "nationalism."

In Chapter III; "Methodology," I discuss the methodology used; a mixed-method approach based upon case study analysis of an individual, semiotic (the study of sign and symbols) analysis, and thematic analysis of speech texts inspired by the methodology of Grounded Theory.

Part 2. History, Power, and Ideology.

In chapter IV; "Malaysia: Geography, Demographics, History, and Politics," I provide Malaysia's geographic, demographical, historical, and political background.

In chapter V; "Malaysia under Mahathir Mohamad," I discuss the state under Mahathir paying attention to the dimension of power maintained by this individual who has ruled Malaysia for 23 years.

In chapter VI; "The Mantra and its Origins: Appropriation of Ideology," I highlight the origin of Cyberjaya and discuss the phenomena of the "Stanfordization" of Malaysia.

Part 3. Inscriptions of Ideology.

In chapter VII; "Inscription #1: Analysis of Select Brochures," using a Semiotics Analysis Approach (Kress & van Leeuwen, 1996; Rose, 2001; van Leeuwen & Jewitt, 2001), I analyze select pages of brochures on Malaysia's Multimedia Super Corridor (MSC).

In chapter VIII; "Inscription #2: Analysis of Speech Texts," I discern concepts such as technological determinism, national strategy, and globalization from select Prime Ministerial speeches as they relate to the development of Cyberjaya and the MSC. I discern the idea of hegemony and draw out its subdivisions to answer the main theme of inquiry of this study on the nature and subdivisions of hegemony and utopianism. Using the software *Atlas ti* (see Muhr, 1997), I analyze data from 21 speeches by going through the process of analysis inspired by the Grounded Theory Method.

In chapter IX; "Inscription #3: Analysis of Landscape," I analyze how the idea of Silicon Valley gets enculturalized and become a model for the development of Malaysia's MSC. I discuss how "large scale" inscriptions of foreign, especially American signs and symbols, become corporate installations or real estate projects that transform the landscape as well as the social relations of production. I analyze photos I took during my fieldwork.

In chapter X; "Inscription #4, Stanford-ization and McDonaldization of Malaysia," again, using select photos taken, I look at how popular American business and consumer cultural symbols are installed onto the landscape and what this means to this study on hegemony.

Part 4. Discussion.

In chapter XI; "Conclusion: On Hegemony and Utopianism," I conclude the study with a discussion of findings concerning the themes of hegemony and utopianism. I draw upon the various sub-findings on the theme of inscription and provide a general explanation of how hegemony particularly operates as technology interplays with culture.

In chapter XII: "General Statements Concerning Language," I describe the propositions generated from the study and situate them within the implications of my findings.

Finally, in chapter XIII; "On Hegemony, Technology, and Authority," I discuss some of the developments of the Multimedia Super Corridor after the retirement of Mahathir Mohamad.

I will now proceed with the second chapter of this dissertation; on the major concept of "cybernetics" and other related ones explored in this study.

Chapter II

REVIEW OF SELECTED LITERATURE

"Success! O you, all the powerful divinities who are assembled,
and who protect [this] province [*kadatuan*] of *Sriwijaya*; you
too, . . . and all the divinities with whom all curse formula
begins!"

—From *The Kota Kapur Inscription* [*of Sriwijaya*], (Coedès
& Damais, 1992, p. 55).

The Mantra of Information Technology
and its Sources

In Sanskrit, the word "mantra" (*mentera* in Malay[5])
means formula. In the context of this study, the mantra
is correlated to the idea of a grand strategy or a belief
system in the form of political ideology that permeates
the consciousness of the leader and the led or the author

---

[5]   Malay or Bahasa Malaysia is the national language of
Malaysia.

and the authored. Inscribed onto the consciousness of the people, *via* print, broadcast, and electronic media is the mantra of economic success rapidized by information technologies. The formula for success many developing nations, such as Malaysia, is undertaking is one characterized by the dependency on Informational Communications Technologies (ICT) particularly on the technology of the Internet/broadband to fuel the engine of capitalist development, relegating the state as a haven for cheap pool of labor in the microchips industry (McMichael, 1996). The mantra of success is one driven by the belief in the formula of "cybernetics." I will discuss how the cybernetic chant, one orchestrated and broadcast by the government, permeates through the social environment.

In this chapter, I shall relate the idea and genealogy of cybernetics to the idea of what is currently known as "Information Age" or its varying and more fanciful terms such as "The Age of Cybernetics," or "The Networked Economy," or "The Digital Age." I will then relate the idea of this "formula" of cybernetics to the notion of "inscription" of the ideology onto the landscape of human consciousness since the beginning of the second half of the twenty-first century.

On Cybernetics

The idea of "Information Society" or "The Network Society" stems out of the revolution in computing and has transformed our psychological, ideological, and material landscape of humanity. Social relations of production are altered and transformed as a result of new patterns of division of labor in what Gleick (1988) would call patterns that arise out of randomness and chaos.

There are different levels of meaning of cultural change as it is impacted historically by "technologies of the body," such as the Internet. In the case of cybernetics as technologies of the mind, this seems to be a "natural progression of late stage of capital formation" and in fact, as Marcuse (1941) and many a Frankfurt School analysts (e.g. Horkheimer, 1973) would call an age wherein technologies are at its final stage of development which will actually liberate humanity out of mundanity as a consequence of automation. Hence cybernetics, as a foundation of artificial intelligence and a philosophy close to the Cartesian philosophy[6] of the mind and appealing to the "philosophy of human liberation via technological feats," is at the present, the highest stage in the development of techno-capitalism. This proposition is reminiscent of Lenin's conclusion on the analysis of capitalism made almost a century ago (Lenin, 1916).

Writings on social structures and political theory have primarily centered on the relationship between Capital, Humanity, and Nature. Many have written on how capitalism appropriates natural resources through the creation of labor and surplus value, which will then establish classes (See Frank, 1966; Wallerstein 1981, 1990; Wignaraja, 1993;) and habitus (Bourdieu, 1994). The debates that rage between the proponents of free market enterprise and command or controlled economies revolve around the issue of human nature, and who gets to control the production and dissemination and the monopoly of capital. At times,

---

[6]   The philosophical foundation of logical-positivism as well as cybernetics can arguably be traced to Descartes (1641/1996) idea of the separation of the mind and body or the doctrine of the duality of the self.

on a different plane there is also the reflection on the need for capital to be interpreted not only as physical or material, but also as cultural, and metaphysical. The central issue of these writings and debate and reflections is of equality and equity; an issue that continues to plague humanity in this age of rapidized technological developments, as echoed by many a contemporary social theorist (Bell, 1976; Ellul, 1964).

In the age of cybernetics, Rousseau's (1755/1992) notion of the discourse on the inequality amongst men[7] can be used to explain the evolution of contemporary social problematique such as digital divide, architecture of power, and the erosion of the Self into fragmented and miniscule selves (Turkle, 1997). Other themes also include the furtherance of protectionist democracy via the use of tools of cybernetics, the control over the coding, encoding, and decoding of information by those who monopolize information, and a range of other tools of imperialism and domination and hegemony deployed and employed to the fullest advantage of those who owns the means of social reproduction. And those who own the means to control these processes can also own the means to engineer cultural reconfigurations (see Adorno, 1991; Chomsky, 1989; Horkheimer, 1973; Said, 1993). The nature of thought formation and consciousness production in the world of broadcast media (Bagdikian, 1983) can be exemplified in the media capitalism of Rupert Murdoch whose empire span Britain and the United States (Fallows,

---

[7] See Rousseau's discussion on the roots of inequality in Rousseau, J. J. (1992). *Discourse on the origin of inequality* (D. A. Cress, Trans.). (Indianapolis, IN: Hackett Publishing Company.) (Original work published 1755).

2003) made possible by the modern oligopolic system of capital accumulation (see for examples, Barnet & Muller, 1974; California Newsreels, 1978 for an early analysis of oligopoly).

The scientific paradigm of cybernetics, by virtue of its origin in the mathematical and exact sciences, out of the Copernican Revolution, of Newtonian physics and of Principia Mathematica, onwards to its march of Classical Physics, and next, Quantum Physics and Informational and Decisional Sciences and so on—is a science which has appropriated the "Natural-ness" of the art of being human. Being a paradigm subjected to the development of propositions, verification by the testing of hypotheses, falsification by the rejecting and accepting of the null, and replicating these processes and so on and so forth (Rosenblueth, Wiener, & Bigelow, 1968), cybernetics creates a "space" between what is Natural and what is Artificial. In-between these spaces, Technology as the motivator of civilizations to progress and to dominate, to extent the limits of what otherwise is impossible (for example the navigational technology of Christopher Columbus which made it possible to open up European colonization of the Native Indians of Amerigo Vespucci's America)[8] is also psychologically, a way to create the Technocratic and Authoritarian self.[9] In between these spaces of Nature versus the Artificial lie Media as technology

---

[8]   For a discussion on the social history of the United States, see for example, Zinn, H. (1980). A people's history of the United States. (NY: Harper and Row Publishers.)

[9]   For a philosophical discussion on the relationship between existentialism and technology, see for example, writings on Martin Heidegger for example, Neske, G., & Kettering, E.

of the mediated self. Technology, as it is developed not by the hands of the "Author" has thence become a powerful tool of the surreal—of inequality amongst men (Rousseau, 1755/1992). Popular culture presents technology as a colonizer of humanity, as exemplified by the theme of the movie, The Matrix (Mason & Silver (Producers), & Wachowski & Wachowski (Directors), 1999).

Cybernetics as a paradigm of thinking about the technology of action and feedback and the loops they produce (see Bertalanffy, 1968; Simon, 1996; Wiener, 1954) is an interesting synthesis of three theoretical orientations: logical positivism, critical theory, and phenomenology (see Bredo & Feinberg, 1982). The paradox is that on the one hand, it is derived from the Classical and Quantum Physics, on the one hand, it is a good foundational philosophy of technologism which combines many fields to form a unified theory of living things (like Critical Theory's attempt to universalize and integrate the disciplines, albeit in a dialectical fashion), and on the other hand, Cybernetics too is phenomenological.

Precisely because we can derive three clusters of theories out of the paradigms above makes Cybernetics appealing and hegemonizing. The Internet as a manifestation of the ideology of cybernetics is a good example of how it is both a technology of advanced logical-positivism, and at the same time, one that is employed to make the concept of democracy more "accessible" when one goes into the study of free speech on the Internet.

(1990). *Martin Heidegger and national socialism: Questions and answers* (L. Harries Trans.). (New York: Paragon House.)

Cybernetics and the Idea of Cyberjaya.

What is the link between the mantra of Cybernetics and the creation of Malaysia's Cyberjaya? In Figure 2, I propose a visual representation of a possible link between Cybernetics and Cyberjaya; on how the idea of cybernetics, as Systems Theory (employed to explain the nature of how living systems operate in a loop-feedback fashion, as Bertalanffy (1968) suggested undergoes transcultural evolution. The idea is now interpreted and transmutated by the government of Malaysia to mean the base and superstructure of hypermodern digital cities such as Cyberjaya, a city that embodies a new spirit of national development. Hence, the term evolved from the description of the physics of living things to the politics of domination and control in what I argue, is commonly known in the world of militarism, as the science of Command, Control, Communications, and Intelligence (C^3I).

Malaysia's economic development follows the path of Western-styled developmentalism and can be characterized as Wallerstein (1981) would propose, attempting to liberate itself from the shackle of dependency of the post-colonial system. The creation of the Multimedia Super Corridor (MSC) (see Multimedia Development Corporation [MDC], 2003) is a testimony of the political leadership's subscription to the Rostowian and many a laissez-faire theorists' model (see for e.g. Rostow, 1960) of economic growth.

Castells and Hall (1994) also wrote about the developmental feature of states undergoing economic transformations as a result of the informational revolution, in what the authors term as the development of "technopoles" or new economic growth centers as a consequence of the computer revolution. The MSC is in fact, inspired by the success of the California's Silicon Valley and Boston's Highway 128 (Castells & Hall).

In the preceding paragraphs, I illustrate the notion of "inscriptions;" how the idea of "cybernetics" drawn from Quantum Physics, gets enculturalized onto the landscape of the Malaysian advanced developmentalist project called "Cyberjaya"—all these under the logical-positivist notion of human and national development.[10]

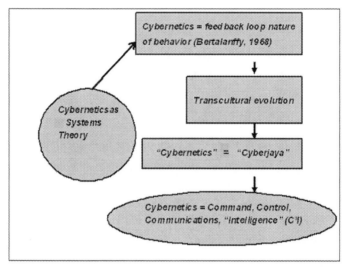

Figure 2: Cybernetics: A Conceptual Transmigration

The paragraphs above, by way of a review of a sensitizing concept, thus represent my early thoughts on the nature of cybernetics. Because my exploration in this dissertation concerns the concept of hegemony that is derived from

---

[10]   See Seers, 1972; and Schultz, 1971 for contending viewpoints on human capital revolution.

cybernetics, a review of this nature is necessary; that genealogy is an essential tool of analysis.

The thrust of the transformation in Malaysia is in the idea of technological, mainly technological literacy, as a vehicle of change and as a new definition of literacy. A key element of the production and reproduction of the ideology of cybernetics as it made possible the creation of the real estate of Malaysia's MSC is education. Whilst Stanford University propelled the growth of California's Silicon Valley and Massachusetts Institute of Technology helped to re-stimulate the growth of The Greater Boston Area (Highway 128), in the case of Malaysia, the establishment of Malaysia's Multimedia University is designed to help the country achieve a similar impact, in an era the economist, Thurow (1997) would call "brain power industries."

On Hegemony

Writings on the idea of hegemony, with its Greek root word "hegemon" meaning "to lead," have mainly been popularly attributed to the work of Antonio Gramsci. For the Italian writer, "hegemony" represents a moment in history, or a "historical bloc" in which the leader (in this case Mussolini,) gains acceptance based on his ability to lead, morally and intellectually (Gramsci, 1971). The status of civil society is achieved when the "masses" or the people led accepted the idea of the ruling class (the regime and its doctrine) as "common sense." The circumstance of the acceptance of this condition, according to Gramsci, is made possible with the dominance of "Fordism"[11] as a common-sensical ideology; of which man's creative instincts are controlled, through a rationalization process ideologized by Fordism and Americanism (Gramsci).

Historically nonetheless, the idea of "hegemony" is certainly not new. Religion, myth, and the supernatural have played its "hegemonic role" in maintaining a "common sensical" view of how human beings should be cast and ordered in the ladder of existence and how to behave or be controlled socially and politically. The idea of the "divine rights of kings" in the Middle Ages, is illustrated in the classic case of France's Louis XIV, "The Sun King" who ruled for 72 years from the age of 4 (Spielvogel, 2003), or universally, as in the case of feudal monarchs in China, Japan, and India. In Marx's later writings (Marx & Engels, 1888/1967), the analyses centered around the relationship between the development of classes to the maintenance of the ideology produced by the ruling class through hegemonic formations that correspond to the mode of economic production. In a similar vein, Rousseau wrote about hegemony in his idea of "social contract" in which the ruler and the ruled is bound by a covenant that would facilitate the maintenance of an orderly society (1987). World systems theorists write about hegemony and hegemonic transitions in the rise and fall of civilizations and in the historical process of capital accumulation (Frank & Gills, 1993). In modern times, besides the Internet, television continues to play its role in maintaining the hegemony of promoting consumer culture and the ideology of the advanced capitalism.

---

[11] Ideology of American production process, coined after Henry Ford of the automobile industry.

In the case of the Malay society, the idea of "hegemony" or "political common sense" can be traced to the myth of the covenant between *Sang Sapurba* (the mystic/ philosopher-king) and *Demang Daun Lebar* (the ruler/ representative of the people) in which the myth states that as long as the leader is just, the people will not depose him (Syed-Omar, 1993). Hegemony is also achieved through the installation, imposition, and inscription of the British colonial mode of production (Buckley, 1984; Tarling, 2001) that put the class of colonial serfs or indentured slaves (padi farmers, tin miners, and rubber tappers) in an orderly and appealing master-serf relationship (Alatas, 1977; Syed-Omar, 1993). Memmi (1957/1965) would term this a classic colonizer-colonized relationship in which colonialism became not only a phenomena of economic exploitation but a complex psychological and cultural construct. Syed-Omar especially analyzed the concept of "*daulat*," which connotes "the divine rights of the Kings" as a hegemonic state of political being-ness wrought upon the Malays, especially during the Malacca sultanate spanning to the present day of the reign of the Constitutional Monarch and the nine hereditary rulers.[12]

If in the days of the Sultanate of Melaka, "*daulat*" plays its role as a hegemonizing strategy similar to that of the concept of the "divine rights of kings," in modern Malaysian political context, the modern state or the "*kerajaan*" (a synthesis of the concept of kingdom and

---

[12] For an elaborate discussion on the nature and role of kingship in Malaysia specifically, as well as on the monarchy system in Southeast Asia in general, see for example Kershaw, R. (2001). *Monarchy in Southeast Asia: The faces of tradition in transition. Politics in Asia series*. New York: Routledge.

statehood) operates to maintain that hegemony. The idea of "*daulat*" is cleverly inscribed onto the consciousness of the Malays. A good citizen is defined as one who is law abiding, God-fearing, and one who pays total allegiance to the Malay sultans or rajas and the Constitutional Monarch such that to question the supremacy of the rule of the Ceremonial King would constitute treason. Khoo (1991) who analyzed the transformation of the Malay society from the times of the Melaka Sultanate to the emergence of the Malay nationalism wrote on the idea of a good Malay subject as one who surrenders total obedience to his/her Ruler (the Sultan or the Raja). The king is said to be "[Allah's] representative on this earth" (Syed-Omar, 1993, p. 45) and thus bestowed upon him is the Divine Rights. Social status is calibrated based on the sophistication of the signs and symbols of the Malay sultanate. For example, royal awards are presented yearly to those who have demonstrated good service and relationship to and in accordance with the specifications and alignments of the Constitutional Monarchical system. Upon receiving these awards, some recipients would even be given honorific title that would elevate their social status; an endowment of symbolic power as a result of the process of accumulation of "cultural capital" (see Bourdieu, 1994).

The notion of the "*daulat*" or the divine sanction still continues to this day. One cannot question the legitimacy of the Malay sultans and rajas and the special rights of the Malays and a legal consequence of this would be among others, one can be detained without trial for a maximum of two years under Malaysia's Internal Security Act (ISA). The rights that came about from the myth now become juridical; as enshrined in the constitution to protect the Malaysia protecting the institution of the Malay Sultanate.

Ahmad (1966) and Maaruf (1984) analyzed the concept of a hero in Malay society in which Hang Tuah, the most celebrated and cultural iconic warrior in Malay history is characterized as one who pledges blind loyalty to the Sultan. The image of the warrior-blind loyalist is well inscribed into the literature and consciousness of the Malays (Salleh, 1999), as powerful as the hegemony of the Hindu epic Ramayana (Buck, 1978) in shaping the development of the Hindu–Buddhist tradition in Southeast Asia (Teeuw, 1979). Today, enshrined is the modern-day doctrine of allegiance to the ruler in the form of the "*Rukunegara*" or the "Principles of the Nationhood."[13] The ideological state apparatuses are employed to advance the economic development of the nation as well as to maintain social order so that the state can continue to pursue its development projects along the lines of State-sponsored capitalism that is increasingly taking the character of the corporation nation-state colored by politics of race; a system that continues to prosper *via* a tight nexus between politics and business (Gomez & Sundram, 1999).

On Utopianism

Malaysia's grand design in the form of economic transformation aided by the communications revolution is a form of utopianism. Anderson (1991) might describe

---

[13]   *Rukunegara*, or literally "Principles of the Nationhood" is a set of declarative statements created after the bloody racial riots of May 13, 1969. It is meant to be the guiding principles to help Malaysia steer peacefully through nation-building.

the project as the creation of an "imagined community," and Postman (1993) might call it a deliberate attempt to create a "technopoly." The idea of utopianism is explored alongside the concept of "hegemony" has its roots perhaps as early as when human beings began to organize themselves into "civilized social groups." But perhaps it is best to begin with the notion of utopia in the writings of Plato especially in his description of a republic ruled by a "philosopher-ruler" or a talented aristocracy who has seen the supreme vision after being educated in the best form of democratic ideals (Plato, 1993). The notion of utopia is also written by More (1516/1999), who expounded on a perfect society governed by those who have evolved into ethical beings and achieved the level of nobility.

Much of the writing on utopianism centered on the idea of ideological migration from a world no longer suited to advance civilization of that particular time and place (Claeys & Sargent, 1999; Manuel & Manuel, 1979). In each society at any historical period, the idea of a "perfect society" played its role as a benchmark of civilization. Perfect societies are imagined, so are those that portray utopias gone wrong—controlled by those who control the technologies of controlling others. Orwell's novel *Nineteen Eighty-four* (1948) is one such fictional example that describes a "dystopia" of a totalitarian regime nonetheless; one in which advanced technology played the role of surveillance in a state run on totalitarian principles in which the individual submits to the all-encompassing power of the "big brother" or the State, in a nation wherein the ideology of "doublespeak" or "contradictions" reign supreme.

In this study on Malaysia as a developing nation in which Islam is the official state religion, it is necessary to analyze utopianism within the milieu of the Islamic idea of the "*ummah*" (which connotes a society of people subscribing to the Islamic faith) in which the state's economic, political, and social development also means the creation of an ideal society based on memory of the glories of the Islamic civilization, particularly the utopianism of *Madinah* (Medina) as an often-cited model of governance of the Islamic *polis*. The nature of utopianism in Malaysia hence is religious, making the Multimedia Super Corridor (MSC) a hybrid of Internet-driven technopoly and Islamic-inspired showcase of glory.

In this dissertation, my exploration, through the findings, will attempt to show the fundamental character of Malaysian utopianism as conceived by its author, Mahathir Mohamad; a utopia run on high-speed Internet access. The character of Malaysian utopianism (which has religious undertones) is also then, the ancilliaric subject of inquiry of this dissertation.

On Technological Determinism

A minor, yet fundamentally related concept that I explore in this study is "technological determinism." It is, the belief that technology is a life force in itself, drives social, economic, and political changes, and becomes a culture (Knorr-Cetina, 1983) that even many social forecaster believe drives global transformations (Naisbitt, 1984; Toffler, 1970). It is a philosophical question with the nature of technology at the center of the inquiry. A survey of writings on this issue can be traced perhaps from Plato's idea of *techne'* (1992/2003) as a fundamental early concept of technics, to those that propose that we are all "being digital" (Negroponte, 1995; Papert, 1999).

Ellul (1980/2003) and Mumford (1966) were amongst the pioneers in the debate on the fate of humanity in the face of the advancement of technology; the former writing mainly in the genre of philosophy and ethics of technological progress, the latter, on the architecture of control and power inherent and embedded in it.

Writings in the genre of technology as deterministic can also be found in the realm of early literature particularly in the Romantic period, with the idea of "Frankenstein" as the embodiment of human creation called technology, ran amok (Bennett & Robinson, 1990). Heidegger (1993/2003) particularly paid close attention to the issue, cautioning us of the specter called "technology" that is haunting humanity.

In addition, writings in the genre of technology and social change particularly with computing technologies, evolved from the early writings on science and technics. These writings propose how we surrender our lives to technology (Reinecke, 1984) in city-states called "technopolies" (Postman, 1993).

In this study of Cyberjaya, a "technopole" by definition (see Castells & Hall, 1994), I will explore the nature of "technological determinism."

On Globalization

In this study, I also look at the nature of "globalization," as a phenomena of the movement of goods, people, services, and ideas as a feature of hypermodernity (Appadurai, 1996,) that creates a "McDonaldized" world system (Ritzer, 1998) and how this concept is perceived in the creation of Malaysia's Cyberjaya as an economic nucleus of the Multimedia Super Corridor (MSC). A plethora of writings has emerged addressing the phenomena of globalization. Foucault (1978) writes about the idea of "Panopticon" as a human condition of being watched like prisoners in a well-designed and well-surveillanced environment in which those in power controls the means of closely observing those that are powerless. The role of surveillance is replaced by systems of control, or the emergence of "biopower" (Hardt & Negri, 2000). In a similar vein, Bauman (1998) also writes about the human consequences of globalization when technology rapidizes the development of social relations, giving rise to a culture of global surveillance in what he called the "opticon-synopticon" dialectic of globalization's consequences.

The nature of globalization is thus, if we take Foucault's metaphor, synthesize it with Bauman's (1998) analysis of globalization, we get the notion that we live in an environment controlled by those who owns the means of media production. In short, we live in a world mediated and hegemonized by the "culture industry" (Marcuse, 1964). In many a writing on "globalization," the issue of "structural violence" (characterized by deep divisions between the economic classes of the peoples of the world) is the central theme (see for e.g. Friedmann, 1992). This view is reminiscence of Harrington's (1977) 1970s analysis of American capitalism and its consequences. Moreover, decades of capitalist expansion since the end of World War II and particularly, since the breakup of the Soviet Union have seen the deep-structuring of the cultural, economic, and political contradictions of globalization. Keen observers of the phenomena have written on the cultural consequences of "late capitalism" (Bell, 1976; Jameson, 1991; Wallerstein, 1981) inspired perhaps by Lenin's

(1916) thesis on imperialism as a logical consequence of capitalism. And some have coined the age of globalization as one characteristic of American hegemony that helped regulate the structural functioning of the American "empire" (Hardt & Negri, 2000).

On Nationalism

The last concept I explore in this study of the relationship between hegemony and the interplay between culture and technology is "nationalism." In the previous paragraph, I discussed the attendant concept of globalization as inseparable from discussions on nationalism. The notion of technological change as it impacts sovereign states, I believe, must be looked at in the context of how states sustain the idea of nationalism as yet another dimension of hegemony. Renan (1990) was one of the earliest to explore the notion of "natio" and how it relates to "nationalism." The French Revolution of 1786 was said to be the womb of the birth of the idea of nation (natio). The technology of language, aided by the system of social reproduction called schooling is employed by the ruling class of every epoch to maintain some sense of nationhood so that the state as a political entity can be sovereign and legitimate. The rise of so-called nation-states particularly in Western Europe, after World War I and in the rest of the world, after World War II with the relative withering of colonialism and the dismantling of colonial empires through the two world wars gave nationalism a sense of ideological strength as a counter-ideology, respectively, to fascism and communism.

Smith and Hutchinson (1995) wrote extensively on the history of nationalism and its relationship to concepts such as supra-nationalism, communism, fascism, millennialism, and utopianism. Contemporary writings on this concept saw further explorations in for example, the idea that nationalism has given rise to communities reliving the past and glorifying the sense of "communal being-ness as a people" in what Anderson called "imagined communities" (1991).

Conclusion

To recapitulate the main idea of this chapter, I reiterate that my focus in this research is to explore the variance of the concept of hegemony and utopianism. My questions are: If we are to speak of hegemony, what might be its subdivisions and its transcultural dimensions? If we are to explain a nation's utopian ideals, as this study is also about, what are its properties?

In relation to the theme of inquiry above, I have attempted to provide some of the main sensitizing concepts central to this study on hegemony. I have provided a review of selected literature on "cybernetics." The genealogy of cybernetics is explored so that we can discern the nature of its transcultural transformation: of the philological dimension of the concept. The idea of hegemony is also reviewed so that we may discover the nature of its properties and dimensions. Concepts such as "utopianism," "globalization," "technological determinism," and "nationalism" are explored as inter-relational concepts to hegemony and utopianism. In the following chapter, we will look at the methodology designed for this study.

Chapter III

METHODOLOGY

"The product of the *bricoleur's* labor is a bricolage, a complex, dense, reflexive, collage-like creation that represents the researcher's images, understandings, and interpretations of the world or phenomenon under analysis."

—From *Handbook of qualitative research* (Denzin & Lincoln, 1994, p. 3).

In this chapter, I discuss the methodology used as well as considerations I made when designing the study. I begin with the choice of paradigm, the description of the nature of fieldwork I was engaged in, the sets of I data collected, and next, the process of data gathering and interpretation. Essentially, this is a semiotic study in which I interpret words and visuals and situate them within the framework of analysis of sign, symbols and signifiers.

Methodological Rationale: On Semiotics

To study the Malaysian MSC with specific focus on the intelligent city of Cyberjaya is a complex task. It warrants a complex mode of analysis that focuses on the role of authoritarianism in relation to the installation of ideological-industrial complexes. In the paragraphs that follow, I outline the development of the study of semiotics.

Much of the writings on the origin, development, and refinement of semiotics lie in the field of linguistics and the study of the way language structures, restructures, or alters reality. Plato's collection of dialogues on Socrates brings awareness to the idea of reality versus appearance in how we conceive and perceive existence. There is imperfection in existence since human beings are thought to live a mediated life. Plato in his work on this subject, especially in *Phaedo* (Plato, 1954/1961) and *The Republic* (Plato, 1993) believed that there is a perfect and an imperfect world known respectively as, Essence and Forms. This theory of knowledge, known popularly as "The Doctrine of Reminiscence" derived from Plato's Allegory of the Cave proposes that humanity is thought to be conditioned by a mediated world of signs and symbols that cloud true consciousness (Plato). The Christian notion of "word becomes flesh" (Rahner, 1985), the Islamic idea that the Koran is a book of signs (Armstrong, 1993; Cleary, 1993; Nasr, 1964; Schimmel, 1985), and that it is believed that the human struggle in this world is a "jihad" or a constant and theologically-demanded struggle against falsehood in accordance with what is decreed by the book of signs, and the Hindu belief that the whole world is a manifestation of the syllable "Om" (Radhakrishnan & Moore, 1957)—all these are the notions of the centrality of signs and symbols in analyzing the phenomena of existence itself, when looked at from the point of view of theology. Hence, the Platonic and religious perspectives of the individual in his/her environment were meant to explain, in genres such as prose and poetry, the forces that define the subjective experience of existence (Abdulla, 2000; Buber, 1958; Kegan, 1982). Writings on the idea of humanity and signs and symbols continue to be produced in subsequent periods having their parallel development in the historical march of literature and philosophy.

Writers in the Romantic tradition, particularly Byron, Keats, Shelley, and Wordsworth write about the superiority of the human intellect, sense awareness, and the Platonic God (Abrams, 1971) poetizing and narrating the predicament and fate of humanity at the advent of the Industrial Revolution. One might argue that the Romantic period in Western literature precursored the age of Western existential thought of which France and French Algeria for examples, became fertile grounds of powerful analyses concerning the subjectivity of humanity in the face of the structures it lives in (Camus, 1975; Fanon, 1967; Memmi, 1957/1965; Sartre, 1975).

In the twentieth century, Humanity as it exists in history and materiality, continues to be a theme of philosophical inquiry. The question of the influence of signs and symbols on consciousness and how they are situated within the material environment the individual is in, is further explored either directly or indirectly especially by existentialist philosophers and writers such as Camus, Kafka, Kiekergaard, and Sartre, (Kaufmann, 1975) and in plays written in the genre of Absurd Theatre by playwrights such as Beckett and Ionesco (Esslin, 2001;

Matthews, 1974).The idea of existentialism and the human condition, particularly concerning the meaningfulness of existence in the face of human conditions such as hunger, poverty, discrimination, war, and oppression as written by French philosophers (e.g. Sartre, 1975) became a common theme of inquiry in the arts and humanities. In much earlier writing on this subject, one can find inspiration from the radically existentialist philosophies that grew from a critique of Marxism (see for example, Bakunin, 1953). In Southeast Asia, works of literature especially in the decades characterized by the struggle against colonialism, reflect existentialist themes that attempt to put the human self as victims of systems of signs and symbols created by those who owns the means of intellectual, cultural, and material production (see for example Rendra,1979; Toer, 1993). Contemporary Marxist scholars continue to link the necessity for the existence of signs and symbols to formation, development, proliferation, and sustenance of ideology (Eagleton, 1991).

As the twentieth century comes to a close, the field of semiotics began to emerge as an analytical discipline in the study of how language liberates or oppresses. One can now be introduced to terms such as "social semiotics," "discourse analysis," "critical discourse analysis," and others that attempt to suggest that researchers look at signs and symbols from a more sophisticated structuralist perspective in order to further understand the human condition particularly in the age of cybernetics wherein raging philosophical debates is taking place on how the self is a product of a mediated process; one that is not only conditioned by the media (Chomsky, 1989, 2001; Gitlin, 1983; Parenti, 1993) but also by the Internet (Turkle, 1997). In the emerging field of Cultural Studies media theorists writing in the tradition of the Frankfurt School of Social Research (Geuss, 1981; Jay, 1973; Kellner, 1989), and those schooled in French Structuralism see the study of humanity in the ideological and built environment as imperative (see for examples Ang, 1985; de Certeau, 1984; Hall, 1993; Jameson, 1988, 1991; Lefebvre, 1996; Williams, 1977). And theorists trained in the Soviet school of "social semiotics" see the field as valuable and inseparable to the study of human beings and cybernetics (Ivanov, 1977). Citing names such as Barzini, de Saussure, Durkheim, Godel, and Pierce as pioneering contributors, Lekomcev (1977) for example, writes about the multivariate fields the study of semiotics has evolved from. It is also believed that the field of semiotics has its origin in the work of the Russian philosopher Volosinov (Eagleton, 1991). Others have written about the study of "texts" as socially discursive formations (see for example Fairclough, 1992); drawing inspiration from literary themes that conceive the human experience as narrative pieces that tells stories with a major plot and countless subplots, or in terminologies popularly known as Grand and Subaltern narratives. In a similar vein, Said (1978) though not necessarily a semiotician wrote on the idea that perceptions can be shaped by one's cultural and ideological backgrounds that consequently shape the production of knowledge, as in the case of the Western perception and conception of the "Orient." Semiotics, nonetheless might arguably begin with the work of Saussure (1916/1983) and is developed further by, amongst major semioticians, Eco (1976) and Kristeva (1980).

My methodology is informed by such development of semiotics described in the preceding paragraphs. In this study, I take the perspective of methodological design from such a notion of "texts" and its inter-textuality as Kristeva (1980) would analyze, and how concepts such as power, language, and action inter-relates. Hence, the methodology employed (see Figure 3) includes the analyses of the political actor, corporate brochures, policy speech texts, and photographs of the physical landscape and inscriptions in the area of the MSC. These are the sources of triangulation I used in this study on the reading of the multi-textual signs and symbols and how they in turn, can and ought to be analyzed for example, as many a Critical Theorist might propose, through the methodological lens of *ideologikritik* (see Habermas, 1971).

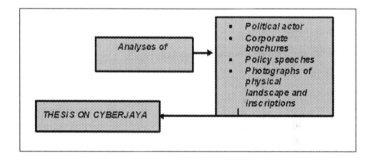

Figure 3: The Study of Cyberjaya

I therefore weave in this dissertation with analyses of these "texts"—from the political actor to the physical landscape and inscriptions"—so that we will not only "read" them, but in the process deconstruct and reconstruct them to answer the fundamental questions raised at the onset of the inquiry on the nature of hegemony and utopianism.

Data gathered

Political Actor: Data on Mahathir.

I gathered information used as data on Malaysia's prime minister who is also the author of the Multimedia Super Corridor, mainly from Columbia University Libraries, in New York City. I also had access to books published in Malaysia written by or about him. The choice of data collected was informed by a research framework known as Gruber's (1989) Evolving Systems Approach for the study of creativity which uses categories known as "facets" to look at the phenomena.

Corporate Brochures.

I collected four promotional brochures concerning Malaysia's Multimedia Super Corridor Project, along with an accompanying Digital Video disc on the MSC, while I was in Malaysia for three weeks in August 2001. They came in the form of a packet containing namely materials meant for international investors. These brochures were recommended to me by officials of the Multimedia Super Corridor (MSC) I met during my fieldwork. The brochures were written in English. They are entitled:

1. "Cyberjaya: The model intelligent city in the making" (Multimedia Development Corporation [MDC], n.d.)
2. "Malaysia in the new millennium" (Multimedia Development Corporation Corporate Affairs Department [MDC CAD], n.d.)
3. "Putrajaya: The federal government administrative centre" (Putrajaya Holdings, 1997)

4. "Unlocking the potential of the information age" (Multimedia Development Corporation [MDC], 1997)

Policy Speech Texts.

In November 2001, I accessed the speech texts from the website of the Prime Minister of Malaysia. These speeches, ranging from 1996 to 2000, contain topics primarily about the Cyberjaya and the Multimedia Super Corridor. I used the search function on the website to narrow my choice to only include speech texts that have the themes concerning Malaysia's technological change. As a result of this narrowing down process, I extracted 21 speech texts delivered by the Prime Minister to a diverse local (e.g. steel factory workers) and international (e.g. investors from Hollywood, California) audience. The speeches were delivered in two different mediums i.e. face to face and through broadcast media.

The speeches were delivered either in Malay (5), English (11), or a combination of both the Malay and English language (5). For speeches that were delivered bilingually, generally speaking, only the opening and closing of the speeches were in Malay. The main speech texts were still written in English. Regardless of the language used, I coded the speeches using the original language they were written in. But for the purpose of reporting this study, selected translations of the texts in Malay is provided. The accuracy of the translations is checked by another fellow Malaysian.

The speeches were downloaded from the website and archived directly into the databank of the Grounded Theory software, *Atlas ti* (see Muhr, 1997). I draw themes and initial codes based on my research questions and sensitizing concepts, analyze them using the software above, and situate them within this study of hegemony and utopianism.

Photographs.

While in Malaysia (in August 2001), I took more than a hundred photographs and even managed to get an aerial view of the Malaysian Multimedia University as I was arriving from the Southern part of Malaysia, en route to the Kuala Lumpur International Airport. I used a digital and a 35 mm camera interchangeably to take select pictures of the landscape of the MSC.

At the onset of the study, I already have an early perspective on what data to choose based on the inquiry theme of hegemony and utopianism. I wanted to look at the signs and symbols in the landscape of the site of the study to discern the signifiers that can be derived. I focused on the signs and symbols that show me the pervasiveness of signs and symbols that are foreign to the culture of the peoples and how these have become architectural landscape and hence a "common sensical" manifestation of the transformation that the nation is undergoing. So, among the sets of photographs that I took were: icons/symbols of American business such as McDonald's, Starbucks, and Hard Rock café, the area of the MSC Technology Park, the Petronas Twin Towers and its surrounding, business billboard on highways, and the campus of the Multimedia Super Corridor. The criteria used for taking the photographs are the ones I call "Stanfordization and McDonaldization of Malaysia" or "Cultural-Industrial Complexes" and "Cybernetics Trickle Down."

Apart from taking photographs of signs and symbols that originate from American corporate interests in the nation, of the English language, and the language of corporate advertising that dominates the country, I also took photographs of the language of change that is being transformed in an educational setting such as the naming of streets on the campus of Malaysia's Multimedia University.

I wrote notes to "read" the photographs as texts (see Figure 4 for an example). Photographs taken with a 35 mm camera were scanned onto diskettes or retaken using a digital camera, and then notes (Observer's Comments—OC) were written beside the picture. The notes also include the date and place the photographs were taken.

The camera I used has a built-in date tracker function. So, the dates the photographs are taken were gleaned from the printed copy of the photographs. I took notes of where the photographs were taken after each site visit. And when the photographs were printed, (usually within 48 hours after they were taken,) I labeled the place the photographs were taken. In addition, identifying the place the photographs were taken was also aided by my familiarity with the places I visited.

Notes and Fieldnotes.

There are two categories of notes I took: notes and fieldnotes. Notes constitute all those taken before and after my field trip. These might not be related directly to the data but made useful to sensitize me to all the aspects of the study. The memoing process in these mini notebooks began even before the proposal of this study was finalized. These were drawn from my own musings on the topic of changes happening in Malaysia, as well as from the many hours of dissertation seminar I sat in Professor Herve Varenne's classes in Anthropology.

Date: August 19, 2001
Place: Malaysian Multimedia University
OC: [Observer's Comments]
Another inscription in the form of a road sign. This road is called "*Jalan Silikon*" or "Silicon Road." Interestingly, the naming of names can be a very significant and fertile research area in the study of discursive formations. It might have been a natural and logical act of naming a road in a Multimedia University campus by the name "Silikon" but there are also hegemonic dimensions to the practice.

Figure 4: Reading *Jalan Silikon*

I also wrote notes and memos in an online discussion board I was actively participating in between May to August of 2001 (see Appendix A for a sample note that was written on September 11, 2001 after I have just returned from my data collection trip from Malaysia). The forum was started by a company, now defunct, called iSMETA, based in Kuala Lumpur, Malaysia in which middle-class Malay professionals that used to be my high school friends use the forum to stay in touch with each other as well as to exchange ideas. The communication channel is called "famili.tv" and anyone can create a free account to communicate with friends or family members. For me, the forum was a perfect opportunity to gather information on the Malaysian thinking of the day concerning the issue of technology and social change, especially on the topic of Malaysian MSC. Since then, I created a special account called "Thesis on Cyberjaya" of which I keyed in my daily thoughts into the electronic discussion board. In general, I took notes on the areas I designated as relevant to my study, namely the area of the MSC such as—Cyberjaya, Putrajaya, the Malaysian Multimedia University (henceforth, "MMU"), The Kuala Lumpur City Center (henceforth, KLCC), and the Petronas Twin Towers.

Fieldnotes are created specifically during fieldwork itself. They can be in the form of "Observers Comments" (OC) or notes to accompany the photographs taken (like the one in Figure 4 above). I took notes daily (see Figure 5 for an example). I would begin with mind maps designed on small notebooks then, within 24 hours expand them into scratch notes and next type them into full length notes to be used in the analysis or constant comparison stages. Figure 5 is an example of a mind map of a fieldwork on Kuala Lumpur's "*Bintang Walk*" and its elaborated version. The title of the mind map is "KL (Kuala Lumpur) Nightlife." This is a popular and busy nightlife street that has a bilingual name. It literally means "Star Walk." It is a place with a wealth of signs that is beginning to signify the "cosmopolitan-ness" of Malaysia's urban life on the one level, and on a deeper level, one that is signifying the varied spaces that are colonized by media power.

Data Analysis Procedures

In the following paragraphs I explain the procedure that I use to analyze the different sets of data collected in this study, beginning with the study of the individual/ political actor as text and ending with the notes I use to triangulate the data.

Political Actor: Data on Mahathir. Gruber and Wallace (1978) write about the meaning of creative development in which it is stated that: development is not restricted to an uni-linear pathway since an evolving system does not operate as a linear sequence of cause-effect relationship but displays, at every point in its history, multi-causal and reciprocally interactive relationships both among the internal elements of the systems and between the organism and its external milieu. (p. 1)

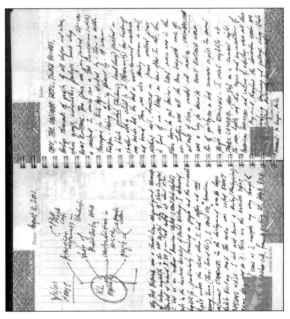

Figure 5: Notes on "KL (Kuala Lumpur) Nightlife"

Indeed Gruber and Wallace's definition as such is pertinent as a basis of studying a statesman whose development must be looked at not only within an important historical context but also contingent upon the subject's own internal systems of thinking as well as the political-economic context the subject shapes and is being shaped. I find it crucial to study the author and the nature of authoritarianism generated in studying hegemony.

In this study, I have used Gruber and Wallace's (1978) concept of "personality as data," where "k" stands for subject and "facets" as categories are used to analyze the individual under study (see Figure 6). The eight facets and their explanation are 1) epitome (achievements); 2) central conflict (inner tension); 3) network of enterprise (the range and interconnectedness of activities; 4) modalities of thought and expression (style of metaphoric thinking); 5) problem-solving (skills used to solve problems); 6) point of view (outlook in life); 7) development (personal and professional development in his/her career); and 8) interpretive work (most important creation). These are the facets that help present a kaleidoscopic picture of the case. I use this approach to analyze the author and the authoritarian personality.

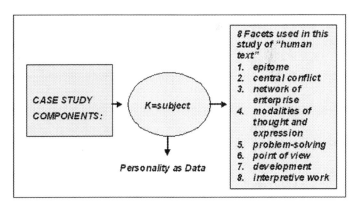

Figure 6: Gruber's Evolving Systems Approach

Corporate Brochures.

Using the semiotic analysis approach, I analyzed select pages of a pamphlet called "Malaysia in the new millennium" (MDC, n.d.). I also analyzed select pages from the brochures entitled "Putrajaya: The federal government administrative centre" (Putrajaya Holdings, 1997), "Unlocking the full potential of the information age" (MDC, 1997), and "Cyberjaya: The model intelligent city in the making" (MDC, n.d.). These are major publications produced by the government to promote the MSC to foreign investors.

In doing semiotic analysis, I would first find out its author and the aspects of the authorship of the brochure produced. I look at aspects such as the corporate authorship, the material it is made of, and the audience they are intended for. I then analyze the images from a universal perspective, or to have a global picture of it in general. I then analyze it in detail, from the analytical perspective. For example, in the case of the brochure on the city of "Cyberjaya," I looked at the images, font, and colors used and speculate the intended effect of the advertising techniques. Some of the images are reproduced for the analysis. I use arrows to point to the analyses made of the images. For most of the images, I use tables with three columns to analyze them from the perspective of "sign," "signifier," and "signified." By sign, I mean the word/ object/symbol itself. By signifier, I mean what it points to and by signified, I mean its mental representation. In my analyses, I am aware of my subjectivity as an interpreter of these signs and symbols. However, since I was brought up in that culture, I believe I have unique insights into the symbolism of the culture and since I have lived in America for a total of thirteen years, I also have a similar insight into American symbolism.

Policy Speech Texts.

Using the software *Atlas ti*, (see Muhr, 1997) I first select the speeches on the Malaysian MSC from the official website of the Prime Minister of Malaysia, load these into the archive of the Grounded Theory software and based on the initial codes created, match the quotations from the text. In other words, I archive the 21 speeches and coded them according to the initial themes I came up with at the onset of this study. The themes are primarily based on the sensitizing concepts discussed in Chapter II of this dissertation, namely "cybernetics," "hegemony and counter-hegemony," nationalism/national strategy," "utopianism," and "globalization." They are designed to answer the question on the variance of hegemony as the theme of inquiry in the case of the Malaysian project. Figure 7 below is an example of a page illustrating a speech text (left column) and its initial codes (right column). Most of the quotations are sentence-long and some have two to three sentences in them.

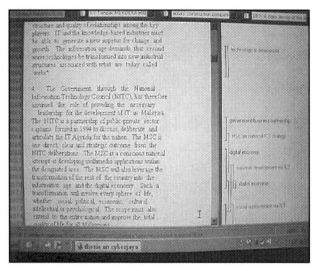

Figure 7: Sample Text and Initial Codes

From the speech texts, I came up with a total of 828 codes that were then reduced to 180 categories that was then further reduced, based on their saturatedness into major themes used to draw the relationships in this study. Over a period of more than a year, I read and reread the speeches and coded themes such that a total of 1342 codings were made for all the 21 speeches.

The most saturated code for example is "Technological Determinism" with 45 quotations attached to it. Figure 8 shows a sample page of quotations derived and the list of codes I used. In this example, there are 45 instances/quotations attached to "Technological Determinism" that appear in all the 21 speeches I analyzed. The dominant theme in the speeches is thus in the belief that technology drives policies more than the idea of human agency. In the Figure 8 below, the numbers on the left represent the sequence of the speech text as it is archived in the software, and the line number in the text. Hence, the number "1:6" means the quotation is derived from the sixth line of the first speech text in the databank. The number on the right (e.g. 39: 43) represents the location of each sentence in the list of hundreds of sentences from all the speech texts archived in the databank of the software.

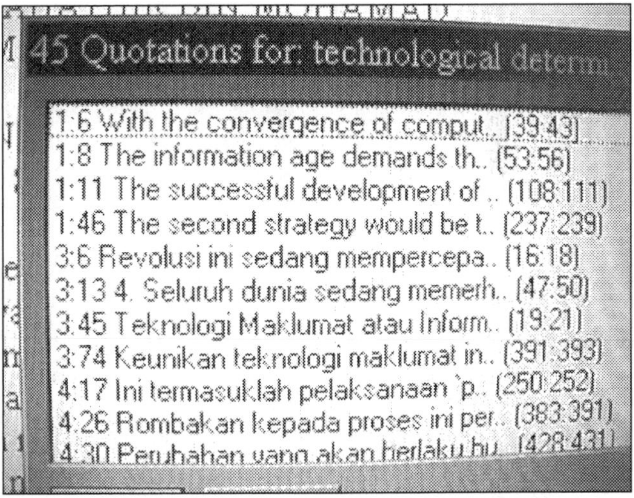

Figure 8: Sample Page of Quotations from a Code

Figure 9 below shows examples of pages on the list of initial codes used to guide me through this Grounded Theory-inspired study. The left panel shows the list of codes used while the one on the right is an example of a drop down menu of the codes and the list of quotations that go with it. For the initial codes on the left, I created subcategories of a code if I feel that there will be many quotations that will emerge during the analysis. Thus, for example, for the quote "digital proletarianism" I have sub-categories such as "digital proletarianism (in general)" "digital proletarianism: rhetoric," and "digital proletarianism: the individual and the state." In this way, I will have a more diverse range of entries (of quotation) that would allow greater possibilities of categorization. Ultimately however, the codes are greatly reduced to a few major ones that draw the relationships between the variables. In the Figure 9 below, on the right shows an example of the code "cybernetics" that has 10 quotations as illustrations.

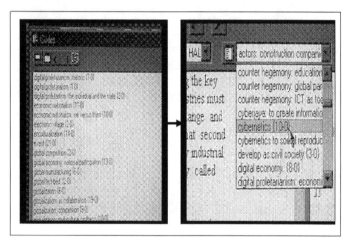

Figure 9: Sample Page of Initial Codes Used and Coding Process

To triangulate the data from the speeches, besides coding, I added theoretical and operational memos to the codes. I came up with 92. Figure 10 below shows a sample page of a reflective memo entry. I used several types of memos namely, "Operational" (to guide me through the next step), "Descriptive" (to explain the quotation presented), "Reflective" (to link the quotation/idea with a body of related work), "Theoretical" (to link an idea with a theory from perspectives such as Structural Functionalism,

Critical Theory, Marxist, Neo-Marxists, and so on); and "Initial Proposition" (to link the idea with theory building and propositions to be developed in the later chapters.) The different types of memos are a way to triangulate the data as guidelined by the Grounded Theory Methodology.

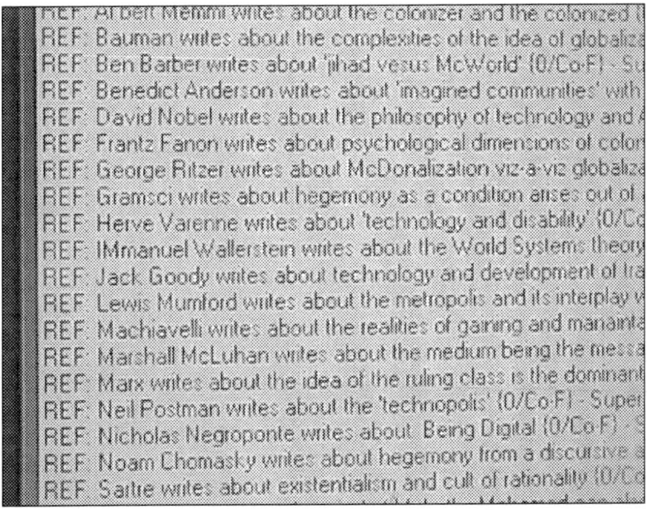

Figure 10: Sample Page of Memos ("Reflective")

Photographs.

I used the semiotic approach to analyze selected photographs that I took. My aim is to draw a composite picture of Malaysia's transformation, bearing in mind the theme of inquiry on hegemony and utopianism and the signs, symbols, and signifiers as analytical tools.

Notes and Fieldnotes.

True to the "constant comparative" method of Grounded Theory, note-taking is an ongoing process. For example, I would look at the mind maps created a year before and reflect upon it in light of new notes created during or even after fieldwork. The point of this exercise is to find consistencies or contradictions in the analysis and to find recurring themes that would then be used to triangulate data gathered from various sources.

Mixed Methodology Approach

In general, I utilized a mixed method approach as reflected in the different chapters I called "analytical." For example, as already mentioned, in looking at the study of authoritarianism in the person of Mahathir Mohamad, I used Gruber's Evolving System's Approach (Gruber, 1989; Gruber & Wallace, 1978) to study 'creativity' that inspired the political will to create the MSC and Cyberjaya. In studying the nation as a whole, I used the lens of political economy, namely Dependency Theory applied to the study of Malaysia's political-economic structure. The theory, popular in the beginning of the 1970s, looks at the unequal relationship between and amongst nations. In looking at the documents and visual data, I used the method inspired by semioticians and Grounded Theorists (Glaser & Strauss, 1967; Strauss & Corbin, 1998).

As Figure 11 below summarizes, data is analyzed in a constant comparison method to generate propositions. Primarily though, the bulk of the analysis utilizes Grounded Theory Method, in which the three levels of findings and analysis are used inductively from data to propositions, from specifics to generalizations, from the categorizing of emerging themes to the drawing of relationships—all these in the spirit of Strauss and Corbin's (1998) "constant comparison" method.

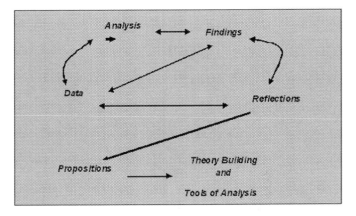

Figure 11: From Data to Propositions to Tools of Analysis

This study is conducted using the mixed method approach as I believe that the theme itself is kaleidoscopic. In other words, I have taken the perspective of what Denzin and Lincoln (1994) call a "bricoleur" in crafting the tools of analyzing the variants of hegemony.[14] Figure 12 below suggests the mixed methodology used, in coming up with a thesis on Cyberjaya. It illustrates how I use different methods of analysis for triangulation purpose; methods such as studying the political actor using the Evolving Systems (case study) approach, studying brochures and photographs using the semiotic approach, and finding

---

[14] Varenne (n.d.) for example mentioned an illustration of the idea of "bricolage" in his example of a French postman Ferdinand Cheval who built his own "palace" out of pieces of stones he collected over a period of thirty years and fashioned it into a mixture of oriental and occidental building.

major themes in the speech texts using a method inspired by Grounded Theory.

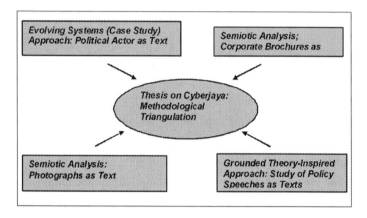

Figure 12: Triangulation in the Study on Cyberjaya

Levels of Findings

There are three levels of findings that I weave into the chapters throughout:

Level 1: General Themes which Emerged.

At this level, I discuss the initial themes of this study, particularly the interplay between "cybernetics" and the local culture in the creation of Malaysia's MSC. I triangulate the notion of the author of the project (The Prime Minister) to illustrate the "human agent"as text. The focus of this level is to draw themes such as "cybernetics," "technological determinism," "hegemony and counter hegemony," "national development strategy," and the "historical naturalness" of hegemonic formation in the case of the creation of the intelligent city of Cyberjaya.

Level 2: Levels of Hegemony and Characteristic of "Utopianism."

At this level, I further explore the character of "hegemony" that emerged out of the textual analyses of this study and juxtapose the discussion with the nature of "utopianism" that is conjured by this Southeast Asian state. I triangulate my methodological analysis with the political economic analysis of the state and draw the dimensions of the concept of "hegemony" using the method of Grounded Theory to further generalize the codes to a level of themes.

Level 3: Propositions on How Nations "Cybernate."

At this level, I use all the data I bound, the codes I analyze, the themes I generate, the initial relationships I draw, and the theoretical and methodological triangulation strategies I employ, to propose how developing nations "cybernate." I generate several propositions to formulate what I call a "Theory of Hegemonic Formations" (at the level of states in a globalized economy).

The three levels therefore, are my strategies of making sense of the creation of Malaysia's MSC.

PART 2

HISTORY, POWER, AND IDEOLOGY

Chapter IV

MALAYSIA: GEOGRAPHY, DEMOGRAPHICS, HISTORY, AND POLITICS

"The nation-king cannot exercise its sovereignty itself; it is obliged to delegate it to agents . . . who seeks to win its favor."

—From The communist manifesto and other revolutionary writings (Proudhon, 2003, p. 117).

In the previous chapter, I discuss the methodology I used in this study, outlining the rationale as well as the procedures I used to explain the phenomena of change. In the following sections, I discuss the background information, namely the geography, demography, history, and politics of Malaysia that will help situate this study of Malaysian transformation.

Geography

Malaysia consists of East and West Malaysia of which the former is an island that also includes the Indonesian territory of Kalimantan and the latter, a peninsula. The South China Sea separates the two land mass (see the map in Figure 13). The country is located on the Southeastern part of Asia, consisting of a peninsula and the island of Borneo that borders Indonesia and the South China Sea, south of Vietnam. Malaysia has a total size of 329, 750 square kilometers. It has a tropical monsoon climate. Its strategic resources are tin, petroleum, timber, copper, iron ore, natural gas, and bauxite.

Figure 13: Map of Malaysia
Source: Central Intelligence Agency (CIA). (2003)

Demographics

The 2002 population of Malaysia is estimated to be about 23 million people, with almost 2 per cent rate of population growth. About 34 percent of its population is between the age of zero to fourteen, almost 62 percent between the ages fifteen to 64, and about 5 percent falls in the category of sixty-five and over. Malays and indigenous peoples collectively termed as "Bumiputras" (literally "Sons of the Soil") consist of 58 per cent of the population, Chinese 24%, and Indians and others 10%. Malay or Bahasa Malaysia is the official language while English, Chinese (of various dialects such as Cantonese, Mandarin, Hakka,

Hainan, and Foochow) and Indian (of the dialects Tamil, Telegu, Malayalam, and Panjabi) and Thai are spoken. In East Malaysia, the languages of the tribes of Iban and Kadazan are spoken. The literacy rate is 83.5 per cent of the total population. The current emphasis in this country's literacy education is on "computer literacy" or the ability to be technologically literate so that the people can fully participate in the "Information Age" and be intellectually resilient enough to participate in the globalization process (Mohamad, 2002).

History

I will now sketch a brief history of Malaysia, particularly of it as a former British colony, to situate the development of The MSC that houses Cyberjaya. Ancient history of the Malay peninsula chronicle the region as a vibrant crossroad of trade called "The Maritime Silk Trade Route" in which the crosswinds help facilitate the maritime trade in Asia (Braddell, 1980; Jacq-Hergoualc'h, 2002). The earliest most powerful kingdom that is linked to the Malays is Sriwijaya (Coedès & Damais, 1992). Arguably, the history of modern Malaysia began with the founding of the kingdom of *Melaka* (Malacca) in the early 1400. Islam, brought to the Malay Islands by Arab and Indian Muslim traders in the 1300s, was the religion of the traditional rulers of the Melakan kingdom and the feudal system was the feature of statecraft. *Melaka* was said to be established by a Javanese prince Parameswara in exile from a power struggle in *Palembang*, Sumatra (Osman, 1997). The prince, before reaching *Melaka*, transited in the island of Temasik, (in what is now the city-state of Singapore,) and murdered the Siamese overlord that was governing the island under a Siamese tutelage system. Escaping to the neighboring peninsula, Parameswara rested under a *Melaka* tree in a spot he came to immediately like after he witnessed a *kancil* (a small reindeer-like animal) overcame a dog. Upon seeing that incident, Parameswara decided to name the declared area of his kingdom, Melaka after the name of the tree he was resting under. Hence generations of the Javanese assassin-prince came to be known as Sultans, ruled the enlarged territory of strategic waterway significant to the growth of the early Malay kingdom (Bastin & Winks, 1979).

The kingdom of *Melaka* was short-lived; the navigational and gun power of the Portugese was more superior to those of the *Melakkans*. The kingdom fell to Portugese rule in 1511. The Portugese possessed superior navigational and military technology, facilitating the conquest of *Melaka*. The date became the earliest of a series of European colonialism. *Melaka*, after the Portugese, was taken over by the Dutch who saw Southeast Asia as an economic region rich in spices (Andaya & Andaya, 1982).

Next came the period of British colonialism. The superior sea power of the British Empire as well as its sophistication in navigational and gunnery technology, fuelled by the Christian military-millinearistic ideology of "Guns, Guts, and Glory," facilitated *Malaya* to be handed over from the Dutch. British rule was the longest of the colonial rules; it left an indelible impact on the historical-materialistic and ideological landscape of the once considered glorious Malay kingdom (Funston,1980; Gullick, 2000; Milner, 1982). The British colonization of Malaya, much like that of the Dutch in Indonesia, the French in Indochina, the Spaniards in the Philippines

(Tarling, 2001), was the feature of nineteenth century imperialism.

On August 31st, 1957 Malaya was officially and peacefully granted independence. It was in September of 1963 that the Federated and non-Federated states of Malaya, Sarawak, Sabah, and initially Singapore united to form what is now known as Malaysia (Funston, 2001; Khoo, 1991; Ongkili, 1985). In 1965 however, the busy port of Singapore, one of the earliest British Straits settlement, ceased to be a member of the Malaysian federation and became an independent city-state. The newly formed Malaysia had to "expel" Singapore for political, geographic, electoral, and demographic reasons—Singapore had too many Chinese that would threaten the new Malay-dominated federation (see for example, Milne & Mauzy, 1999). There were several reasons why the British gave Malaysia its independence. One is that it is costly for the Britain to maintain the states because of the growth of Malaysia's population, and the ailing British Empire saw that it was no longer profitable to maintain colonies.

Furthermore, the attractive idea of self-determinism was gaining momentum especially in the form of nationalist struggles, armed or un-armed, all over the world, with the Beijing-based Marxist-Leninist inspired Malaysian Communist Party as an example of anti-colonialist and anti-imperialist armed struggle (Chin, 1994). In Malaysia, education in various forms was beginning to produce people within each of the ethnic communities not content to leaving their future entirely in British hands. Anti-colonialist attitudes were stirring in the 1930's, heralding strong Malay political organization later (Khoo, 1991; Milne & Mauzy, 1986).

Independence was granted also when the natives were perceived as already been given enough skills and training to govern the country albeit in the style of British colonial administration known as the Civil Service. Many from the aristocratic class went through the process of education for social and political enculturalization through the British education system. Sons of the Malay sultans were sent to Britain to pursue studies in law and administration. In Malaya itself, English-medium (known as "English-type") schools proliferated in all the states paving way for a systematic form of education for social reproduction and for the continuation of British Imperialist ideology. In other words, the structuring of hegemony or the inscribing of the ideology of colonialism at the level of education of the nations was a feature of the strategy of British imperialism (Heussler, 1981; Stockwell, 1995).

An important consequence of colonialism was thus the creation of a class of administrative elite among the "Sons of the Soil": or the *Bumiputras* out of the sons of the traditional Malay Sultans. Malaysia's first Prime Minister, Tengku Abdul Rahman Putra Alhaj, son of the Sultan of Kedah, was educated in Britain. Trained in the British Administrative tradition, he governed like a British official inspired by Malay nationalism couched in British idealism inscribing British tradition of civil service onto the minds of the traditional people. Malaysia's second Prime Minister Abdul Razak, and the third Prime Minister, Hussein Onn, was also British-educated. Malaysia's fourth and recently retired (on October 31st 2003) Prime Minister, Mahathir Mohamad, is the only Malaysian Prime Minister that was not British-educated (see Cheah, 1999). The education of Mahathir Mohamad and the system he evolved through, has contributed much to the manner the state's development policies were engineered, illustrated in his early writings on society, politics, and education (Mohamad, 1995). His fondness of "Looking East," i.e. his deep admiration of the Japanese and "Buying British Last" and his suggestions of creating an "East Asia Economic Caucus" (EAEC) are among the slogans and proposals used to create a sense of identity in the few decades after Independence (Milne & Mauzy, 1999). It is against this backdrop of this Malaysia's fourth Prime Minister, and his administration's coming back to "Asian values" whilst at the same time, seeing the power of Information Technology that the MSC was created (Moggie, 2002).

Politics

As mentioned earlier, Malaysia was granted independence on the 31st of August 1957 and was established as a Federation on July 9, 1963. Its political system is one of Constitutional Monarch, fashioned after the British monarchy and Parliamentary systems, understandably because of the influence of British colonialism. It has nine hereditary rulers in charge of religious and ceremonial affairs to safeguard the interests and rights of the Malays. The hereditary rulers elect their Supreme Ruler or the *Yang Di Pertuan Agong* every five years (CIA, 2003). The head of state functions as a rubber stamp monarch to facilitate the operations of the State. The parliamentary system is bicameral, consisting of a non-elected Upper/ Senate/*Dewan Negara* and an elected Lower House/House of Representatives/*Dewan Rakyat*. There are thirteen states and two federal territories (of Kuala Lumpur and Labuan). The newest federal territory is the city of Putrajaya, an ancillary subject of this study (CIA).

At present, the National Front (Barisan Nasional) which consists of a coalition of communal/ethnic-based political parties has ruled Malaysia since Independence. The United Malays National Organization (UMNO) dominates the coalition that consists of The Malaysian Chinese Association (MCA), The Malaysian Indian Congress (MIC) and other ethic-based parties from East Malaysia (Mauzy, 1983). The leader of the coalition has traditionally become the Prime Minister. At the time of the writing of this dissertation, an alternative coalition, called Barisan Alternatif, was formed out of three parties namely Malaysian Islamic Party (Parti Islam Se-Malaysia), National Justice Party (Parti Keadilan Malaysia), and the Malaysia People's Party (Partai Rakyat Malaysia). It is expected that the coming general election of December 2003 will see the communal-based ruling coalition party being seriously challenged by the new opposition-coalition that aspires to create a new politics organized not along communalism but on social justice, human rights, and inter-racial understanding. The unresolved multivariate issues concerning economic development, democracy, human rights, communalism and class politics will be the areas of contestation of the politics of this nation (Said & Emby, 1996).

Conclusion

In the preceding sections, I have briefly outlined the geographic, demographic, historical, and political aspects of Malaysia. These provide a background to this study of a nation with almost eighty percent of its economy engaged in service and manufacturing, a transition from the agricultural-based economy. The history of the nation is characterized by periods of transformation from one political entity to another: overlordship, kingdomship, colony, to self-government and sovereign state integrated into the closely-knit global production system. In the following chapter, I shall detail the development of the MSC. The medical doctor turned politician became the Prime Minister of Malaysia on July 16, 1981 (i.e. for more than 22 years) in a Malaysia that has been independent for only 46 years. He finally retired on October 31, 2003.

Chapter V

MALAYSIA UNDER MAHATHIR MOHAMAD

"In the land of the blind, the one-eyed man is king"

—H.G. Wells, quoted in McDermott & Varenne (1995)

Introduction

In this chapter, I use Gruber's (1989) approach called the Evolving Systems Approach to analyze Malaysia's Prime Minister, Mahathir Mohamad as a political actor and a text to be read, constructed, and deconstructed. It will be a research approach to study the nature of authoritarianism of the author of Malaysia's "technopole" and how it is possible for the people of Malaysia to be hegemonized by his 22-year rule as prime minister. In the tradition of Gruber and Wallace's research strategy, I will refer to my "text" or my research subject as "K" (K=one case= Mahathir Mohamad). I use eight (out of ten) facets of the system, namely, "epitome," "central conflict," "network of enterprise," "modalities of thought and expression," "problem-solving," "point of view," "development," and "interpretative work," to analyze this author of Malaysia's transformations. Figure 14 below summarizes the 8 facets.

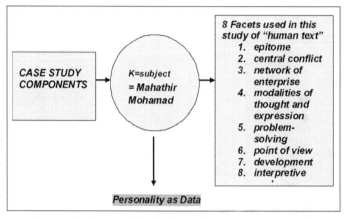

Figure 14: Facets of Gruber's Evolving System Approach

The facets or creative domains outlined above illustrate K's level of achievement. They are looked at within Gruber's proposition to include "novelty," "value," "purpose," and "duration" in the study of creative products. The novelty aspect lies in K's conjuring up of ideas for social transformation which gives value to the nation; these ideas implemented with a sense of purpose over the duration of a long period of time.

Facet 1: Epitome.

"Epitome," the first facet, can be defined as "achievements." Before outlining K's epitome, it is important to chronicle his brief profile as it relates to his political career. K's achievement lies in his success in transforming the people's social, economic, cultural, educational, and political-emotional state of being, i.e. to bring them out of the shackles of colonialism even after the British has granted independence. K was able to bring a sense of unity to the peoples of Malaysia which consist of radically different races—the Malays from the Malay archipelago (and considered the "definitive peoples"), the Chinese from Southern China, and the Indians from Southern India—all whom would have otherwise been difficult to co-exist as a group of peoples called Malaysians. K engineered the thinking of these diverse groups of people into emphasizing their Malaysian-ness rather than identifying themselves through their different ethnic origins.

In addition, K's achievements in the field of economics, in reengineering Malaysia's economic system through systematic five-year Malaysian Plans (national strategic planning like the Soviet Union's system), have brought changes to the use of the nation's wealth and has placed the country as one of the fastest growing economies in the Southeast Asia region. K has been called the "Father of Modern Malaysia." This country is often quoted as a good model of economic development amongst the developing countries.

K's achievement in the field of culture and education lies in his improving of education, raising literacy standards, building better schools, and using printed and electronic media in promoting a culture of learning—all these illustrated his creative work, synthesizing the best of systems from the United States, Britain, Europe, and Japan—so that the nation can be ready for the demands of globalization. Education and social improvement such as total alleviation of poverty are given the highest priorities in the five-year strategic plannings and K's goal is to transform the country into a haven of regional educational exchange so that the country will be as advanced as the industrialized nations. Such a goal, according to K, is to be achieved with a concoction of technological progress guided by morality.

K's achievements in foreign relations (see for example, Pathmanathan, 1990) have also been well-documented in the international media; he is well-known as an outspoken leader of the Third World. K has worked for the regional economic cooperation, championed for nuclear-weapons-free Southeast Asia, sent troops to Namibia and Bosnia for peacekeeping, proposed and pushed for reforms in the United Nations and the Organization of Islamic Countries, helped underdeveloped nations restructure their economy, and called for an "Asian Renaissance" in which the major religions of Southeast Asia would come together to set a peaceful agenda for Southeast Asia in the twenty-first century.

Perhaps the most important achievement has thus far been K's political philosophy and strategic planning for the nation written in a document known as "*The Way Forward-Vision,*" now popularly known as *Vision 2020*; an agenda for national progress and mindshift, which K has commanded the nation to adopt in order for Malaysia to survive in an increasingly challenging world. K's *Vision 2020* outlined several principles of sustainable development in all sectors.

Facet 2: Central Conflict.

The next facet, "central conflict," deals with the subject's sense of rebelliousness. K's central conflict and dilemma lies in his pre-occupation to liberate the mind of Malaysians from the shackles of neo-colonialism. He sees it as an unending struggle to free his people so that they can reach the level of industrial advancement to that of the advanced nations such as the United States, Britain, and Japan. His struggle, more so than that of his predecessors, is also personal as he tried to resolve his anger against colonialism and its consequences. Adshead (1989) explained:

> During the Japanese occupation of Malaysia, from 1942 until 1945, the young Mahathir saw Malays, in his own brothers and cousins included evicted from the employment from Government service clerks and forced to earn a meager living hawking fruits along the roadsides. Mahathir's schooling was suspended from the duration of this occupation, and he had to work in a coffee stall, and to sell bananas in the weekly market in the town which he lived. (p.1)

K was preoccupied with his struggle, leading him to enter politics at a very early age after finishing his secondary school during the years of the Japanese occupation and at the early stage of the return of British rule in Malaya. As written by a biographer:

> Mahathir's political career was therefore launched while he was still at school. In his forthright way, Mahathir looked at the long term position, and recognized that he must become someone of importance and high standing within his own community if his political aspirations is to be

realized. Two professions would enable him to do
this: law and medicine. (Adshead, 1989, p. 33)

K chose medicine over law and it is this profession later
in his development as a politician which has contributed
much to his modality of thought in his observation
of his society, diagnosing its ills, and administering
prescriptions. K's writing illustrating his observations
of the "post-colonial" disease plaguing his people can
be analyzed in his 1970 work called *The Malay Dilemma*
(Mohamad, 1970); a critique of the leadership of the first
Prime Minister. In it he outlined what needed to be changed
in order for Malaysia to continue to exist in a harmonious
state after the bloody May 13, 1969 race riots between the
Malays and the Chinese. The book was banned for several
years and was only allowed to be circulated after K got
into power. Prior to this, K was expelled from the ruling
party of which he had been a member since 1946.

K's work sixteen years later called *The Challenge*
(Mohamad, 1986), further analyzed the continuing struggle
for Malaysia to survive in the 1980s in a world divided by
Cold War political ideologies, and at home, the economic
imbalances which primarily needed to be addressed. His
1991 writing, in the form of a document called *The Way
Forward – Vision* (*Vision 2020*) illustrated his view of some
of the successes his government has made and outlined
bigger challenges for Malaysia to develop in its own mould
in a world economic system characterized by chaos and
competition.

K's *The Way Forward – Vision* (*Vision 2020*)
(Mohamad, 1991), is a document which outlined nine
challenges to be met in Malaysia's journey towards
becoming a fully-industrialized nation by January 1,

2020 This document illustrates K's pre-occupation with nation-building through the constructing of a futuristic mindset.

Thus, the Evolving Systems Approach-Case Study (ESA-CS) of K's creative endeavors in social transformation can be analyzed by looking at the milieu, i.e. the context of post-colonial dilemmas of nation-building and K's involvement as a process and a change agent, looking at his political philosophy as both a process and a product.

Facet 3: Network of Enterprise.

The facet "network of enterprise" explains the series of projects this subject of study engages in. How do we describe K's "network of enterprises"? Gruber and Wallace's (1978) could provide a starting point in analyzing K's system of goals:

> [T]he course of a single project is hierarchically organized: projects, problems, tasks . . . an enterprise is an enduring group related activities aimed at producing a series of kindred products. An enterprise embraces a number of projects. Most typically, as one project is completed, new possibilities come to the fore, to be undertaken next or later. Finishing a project rarely leads to a state of rest; rather it triggers further work as if completion furnishes the momentum to go on. Thus each enterprise is self-replenishing. (p. 23)

It is believed that K is a political workaholic whose array of projects has kept Malaysians labor harder since he assumed leadership. One surprise after another has come up for the last two decades. K's major venture is the creation of The Malaysian Multimedia Super Corridor (MSC), the subject of this dissertation. This creative endeavor is a magnum opus of K's work in the area of infrastructure development and in line with the aspirations outlined in K's document, *Vision 2020*.

Thus, a common pattern in K's creative work as a state leader is his designing of master plans in the areas known to his profession as a national leader. As in Darwin's passion for keeping notebooks, K keeps little notes in which he outlined observations, problems, and solutions to the things he has planned to transform. As noted by Adshead (1989):

> Dr. Mahathir's little notebook is a legend among members of the Cabinet. His critics use this as an example of what they feel to be Dr. Mahathir's over involvement in details of administration. However, he is totally accessible . . . He listens to what people say and makes his own observations. These are then brought to the attention of various Ministers to check and examine—grouse against red tape, condition of public facilities, street lights that are not working, new ideas that strike him as he travels abroad. These jottings represent his total commitment to his work. (p.168)

When he is not working on administrative matters he attends to his hobbies. The latter became an important source of insights into his system of thinking. Mahathir is one who loves cooking, interior designing, woodworking (he has even built his own boat), horse-riding, traveling, and also poetry—writing. It can also be analyzed that through these activities, we can find symbolic manifestations translated from the personal to the public and professional domains in the form of significant projects he has initiated through his long years of leadership. I will discuss this concept of how his hobbies have influenced his public life in the next facet. I now turn to the discussions of K's modality of thought and expressions as it relates to the Evolving System's Approach.

Facet 4: Modalities of Thought and Expression.

In this facet, "modality of thoughts and expression," refers to the system of decision-making and metaphoring the subject operates through. As explained earlier, by training, K is a physician and looks at the society as a patient to be diagnosed and to be administered prescriptions, therapies, or even when the situation demands, to be performed minor and major operations on. In his own words, K related politics with his medical training:

> The first lesson is the methodical way that doctors approach medical problems. Observance, history taking, physical examinations, narrowing the diagnosis and then deciding on the most likely diagnosis and the treatment required. These are useful in any problem in life, and they serve me well in attending top political problems . . . The sense of compassion and the deep understanding that a doctor develops towards patients are also useful in politics. An ability to look at the other side of the picture, the patients' or the opponents' side enables understanding and appreciation. Counter-measures can be developed . . . If the ailments of a society or a nation are attended to in the same way as the illness of a patient, some good results must follow.

The essential thing is to develop diagnostic skills.
(Adshead, 1989, p. 53)

It is logical to explain K's preoccupation with looking at Malaysia as a patient in an Intensive Care Unit (after May 13,1969 bloody riots) on a long road to recovery both physically and emotionally. This too is a powerful metaphor out of which K's political thinking emerges. It can explain a great deal how K has, in his twenty-two-year rule managed to in a manner as a physician, amputates a cancerous organ. This metaphor explains K's survival as one of the longest-reigning Third World Prime ministers of the twentieth century.

Other modalities of thought and expression, which have become second nature to K's mode of thinking, can be analyzed by taking into consideration his hobbies. If in physicianship he acquired the skills of diagnosing and remedying society's ills and engineer its program of well-being, cooking is a metaphor for his ability to synthesize ideas and experiment with recipes for national progress; woodworking lets him imagine nation-building as a tedious and artistic endeavor; interior designing allows him to visualize and beautify space for habitats, horse-riding puts him in a frame of mind of a horsemen and a shepherd to those he is entrusted to lead; traveling widens his horizon and opens up frontiers for new ideas and for making new friends; and last but not least, poetry writing sets his mind to be in reflective and interpersonal moods.

As it relates to the discussion on network of enterprise, if there is an ensemble of metaphors by which we can analyze K with, it is a mix of K as a surgeon-anesthetist, a captain of industry, a school headmaster, an Asian

Machiavelli, a Zulu warrior, a company Chief Executive Officer, a don of a political underworld and a rebel who finds new causes. All these metaphors offer a holographic and panoramic view of his modality of thought and expression applicable to different situations.

Thus, the sum of modalities of K's thought, symbolically manifested through his undertakings either as a profession or as a hobby have been used in his major creative work of governing the nation. Unconsciously or subconsciously, K's creative endeavors have been a series of metaphors. These metaphors become inspirations for K's creations and these "intelligences" become crystallized. They relate to Gruber and Wallace's point regarding " . . . one hardy perennial group of questions concern [ing] the modality in which the creator thinks (1978, p. 20). And K's ensemble of metaphors, as written above, "represent[s] a field of meaning." Through the development of one metaphor to another K, in his days as a politician, much of the progress he has brought to the nation can perhaps (scientifically through the ESA-CS method,) be explained phenomenologically through our analysis of K's inner world.

Facet 5: Problem Solving.

A central aspect of the study of creative individuals in the Evolving Systems Approach is problem solving. Contemporary definitions of creativity and the creative individual continue to highlight aspect of creating new domains, Csikszentmihalyi (1996) notes that:

> Creativity is any act, idea, or product that changes an existing domain or that transforms an existing domain into a new one. . . . [and] a creative person

is: someone whose thoughts or actions changes a
domain, or establishes a new domain. (p.28)

The above definition is consistent with Poincare's
definition of creativity as a process which:

[c]onsists of making new combinations of associative
elements which are useful . . . Among chosen
combinations the most fertile will often be those
formed of elements drawn from domains which are
far apart. (Ochse, 1990, p. 210)

Within the context of the evolving systems approach,
we can further understand problem solving and creativity
within the domain of criteria outlined by Gruber as
having novelty, value, purpose and duration (Wallace &
Gruber, 1989).

Indeed it is not merely sufficient to solve problems but
to fashion products or implement ideas to reach the ultimate
aim of the process of problem-finding and problem solving
in one's creative act. In the case of scientific creativity, the
subject of study may be defined as one who seeks to, in the
former, test hypothesis, and conjure theories which can
paradigmatically shift the thinking in that particular field.
In the case of artistic creativity, the subject may also be
considered as one who attempts to create something new
or establish new genres, which calls for a new definition of
what is discovered. Elaborating on the above perspectives
on creativity, Gruber and Wallace (1978) write:

Generally speaking, people think in order to solve
problems. The excellent problem-solver may have
gotten beyond that point: problem solving comes

relatively easy. It may be apt to say that the creator
sets himself or herself problems in order to think. The
creator is not necessarily a better problem-solver.
The main point is to develop a new point of view, a
perspective from which new problems are seen and
old ones are seen in a new light. (pp. 30-31)

In this chapter on Mahathir's evolution as a thinker,
I find several illustrations in K's work, which almost
correspond to Gruber and Wallace's claim. In the analysis
of K's writing, one can find major instances in which
the opening paragraph suggests K's "problem-finding"
capability becomes relatively at ease in solving them,
and arguably, does "not necessarily [make him] a better
problem-solver" but helps him develop "points of view"
at the peak of his career. But before I venture into the
discussions of the evolution of K's problem-solving facet,
a brief mention of problem solving in the political domain
needs to be made in order for one to find its similarity
in other domains such as in the artistic and the scientific
domains. I refer to the enterprise as a political imagination
and social invention.

Political imagination cannot be any different from
an enterprise of problem solving, problem finding, and
paradigm shifting. Manifestations of the end product may
be looked at in the form of social inventions, which have
their utilities in improving (or destroying,) the lives of a great
number of people. Ideas for social improvements be they,
in the political, educational, cultural or scientific spheres
may be first accepted (or decreed to be accepted) by the
peoples whom the national leader governed and perhaps,
if these ideas are of appealing quality, may be accepted by
peoples outside the territorial states or boundaries. One

such idea may be that of a bank for hard-core poor *(The Grameen Bank)* established by Yunus (Friedmann, 1992). Others of such magnitude coming from political will is that of Gandhi's *satyagraha* (non-violent movement) which have been duplicated by revolutionary leaders worldwide. We saw this in Mandela of South Africa, Aquino of the Philippines, and of Dr. King Jr. and Malcolm X of the U.S.A.

The typology of the creative process described above is described by Wallas, and quoted by Ochse (1993). The four stages include "(1) *preparation*; (2) *incubation*; (3) *illumination*; (4) *verification*." Ochse also mentioned a pre-stage "problem-finding" (p.185) which "has recently become the subject of special psychological study" (pp.186-187). We now look at the analysis of Mahathir as a problem solver in light of the typology mentioned above.

K's identification of problems in his society and ways to act upon them are manifested in a spectrum of illustrations not only from his solution to the attack by currency speculators on Southeast Asian currency (July 1997 to around the year 2000) but also even before his critical and considered controversial analysis of his society in *The Malay Dilemma* in the 1970s. The problems he presented and the solutions proposed as mentioned earlier, led to the banning of the book for ten years; only to be lifted by K himself when he became Prime Minister. His writings before *The Malay Dilemma* have been in the form of newspaper articles, on the need to improve the thinking of the Malays, contributed to the *Sunday Times* between 1946 and 1950.

K's identification of the problems of the Malays, in the interpretation of the May 13, 1969 race riots, is best illustrated in his opening chapter of *The Malay Dilemma* written after his expulsion from the ruling party. His diagnosis of the bloody riots is as such:

> What went wrong? Obviously a lot went wrong. In the first place the government started off on the wrong premise. It is believed that there have been racial harmony in the past and that the Sino-Malay cooperation to achieve independence was an example of racial harmony. It is believed that the Chinese were only interested in business and the acquisition of wealth, and the Malays wished to become Government servants. These ridiculous assumptions led to policies that undermined whatever superficial understanding between the Malays and non-Malays. On top of this the Government glorifying in at it either the opposition or its supporters. The gulf between the government and the people widened so that the Government was no longer able to feel the pulse of the people or interpret it correctly. It was therefore unable to appreciate the radical change in the thinking of the people from the time of the Independence and as the 1969 elections approached. And finally when it won by such a reduced majority the Government went into a state of shock which marred its judgment. And so murder and arson and anarchy exploded on 13 May 1969. That was what went wrong. (1970, p.15)

Quite clearly illustrated as K's problem-finding statement in his first major (and controversial work) lies in the beginning of the paragraph "What went wrong?" and re-iterated with a punch at the end. "And so murder and arson and anarchy exploded on 13 May 1969. That was what went wrong" (Mohamad, 1970, p.15).

It illustrates the beginning of K's style of reasoning throughout his career. The quote on "what went wrong?" thus illustrate the premise upon which K based his analysis of the economic backwardness of his people and how remedies should be prescribed. K sets himself such a problem not only in order to make him think, but to make his reader aware of the issue. His point of view developed out of his paradigm guides the policies to be made in national development.

Sixteen years after K wrote *The Malay Dilemma*, he began his second major work, *The Challenge* with a simple style of problem posing. If in *The Malay Dilemma* the problem was with the Malay's economic backwardness under the rule of its first Prime Minister Tengku Abdul Rahman, in the *The Challenge*, the problem is with the Malays themselves under his rule who opposes his ideas on national progress. K wrote:

> The Malays have emerged from a long period of backwardness only to be pulled in different directions by conflicting forces, some of which seek to undo whatever progress that has been made and plunge the entire community into the Dark Ages. (Mohamad, 1986, p.i)

After consolidating power for the second term, and after narrowly winning the seat in the 1986 General Election in which the Islamic fundamentalist opposition party gained a considerable win, K's main criticism was directed at the "Malays who leaned closest to Islamic fundamentalism" in which the problem identified was of their inability to differentiate what is truth and what is not in the religion. K wrote:

> One of the saddest ironies of the recent times is that Islam, the faith that once made its followers progressive and powerful, is being invoked to promote retrogression which will bring in its wake weakness and eventual collapse. A force for enlightenment, it is being turned into a rationale for narrow-mindedness; an inspiration towards unity, it is being twisted into an instrument of division and destruction . . . Ignorance of what constitutes spirituality, and a failure to see the distinction between materialism and healthy involvement of worldly concerns, render some sections of the Malays (Muslims) community susceptible to the notion that Islam exhorts believers to turn their backs on the world. (Mohamad, 1986, p.ii)

K's opening chapter did not only find the fundamental Muslims as a problem but also in addition to these people, others who are opposed to the ruling party as well. He added:

> At the same time, other sections of the community are being confused by attempts to equate Islam with socialism, using the ambiguity inherit words like justice, equality and brotherhood. (Mohamad, 1986, p.11)

K's preoccupation with the progress of his nation right till the close of the last century with the major collapse of the country's stock markets (along with other Southeast

Asian nations') has shaped his manner of problem-finding in such a way that problems are always seen as coming from outside of him; in the 1970s it was from the then prime minister who ostracized and exiled him, in the 1980s it was from those who opposed him, and in the 1990s it is from "forces" outside of this country, an in the new century, from "European and Jews." In fact, when he was writing for the *Sunday Times* in the 1950s, the problem identified was with the British colonials. I shall elaborate on this paradigm of thinking in the section on K's point of view.

One must bear in mind that, in this life-history method, of studying K, the father figure is dominant in K's life in which K was brought up in a home environment of strict discipline which can explain K's brand of authoritarianism in running the nation and in his style of dealing with his critics. As one who grew up without much inclination to socializing, K has developed a political style of problem solving which illustrates indifference and projects the Machiavellian image. *Asiaweek*, described the link between K's style of leadership and his childhood in that:

> Looking from a telling insight into the political style of Mahathir Mohamad, some analysts like to point to his childhood days. At school, they say knowingly, he was a loner: not given to mixing, always hanging around at the back when the team games were being organized. In adulthood, they like to add his favorite hobbies have included riding and sailing—again, relatively solitary activities. And ones that require keeping an eye on the horizon. (Mitton, 1997, p.1)

It may perhaps be because of his "loner" attitude which has contributed greatly to his ability to objectivize problems and deal with them in manners which are oftentimes contrary to the demands of democratic principles. Thus, K uses whatever means necessary, using his own logic, paradigmed after his "doctoring view, and being unrestrained in his actions, to stay in power and to maintain stability" in the country. Illustrative of his skill in "objectivizing" and "solving problems" is his 1987 decision to arrest and jail without trial those who opposes him. Khoo (1995) for example, wrote about the 1987 mass arrest:

> On Tuesday, 27 October 1987, the police launched *Operasi Lalang* [Operation "Weed Out"] within the first day, *Operasi Lalang* made fifty-five arrests, all under the ISA [Internal Security Act which provides detention <u>without trial</u>] of DAP (Democratic Action Party) MPs, a DAP state assemblyman, second echelon MCA (Malaysian Chinese Association) leaders, Chinese educationists, prominent NGO figures, and university lecturers. Three newspapers, *The Star*, *Watan*, and *Sin Chew Jit Poh*, were suspended indefinitely. Over the next few days, more people were arrested, including politicians from Pemuda UMNO (UMNO Youth) ... Gerakan, PAS (Malaysian Islamic Party,) and the PSRM (Malaysian Socialist Party,) local Muslim teachers, members of some Christian groups, and other NGO activists. The arrests spread geographically from Peninsular Malaysia to Sarawak where local environmentalists and anti-timber logging natives were also detained. The waves of arrests, though lessening after October,

> continued until the number of detainees reached a
> peak figure of 119 in December. (pp. 284—285)

Such is a manner the doctor-politician administered his surgical skills in order to suppress the growth of "political tumor" so that his "capitalist-corporatist developmentalist" plans can be continued and his power maintained. The last episode of a remarkable exercise of such skills is in the expulsion of his deputy prime minister and Prime Minister apparent, Anwar Ibrahim who is now serving a fifteen-year jail term on charges of sodomy, corruption, and abuse of power.

To conclude this section on K's problem-solving skills, I write on how K relates medicine and writing to Sherlock Holmes-type of investigation. He writes:

> . . . it is easy for me to examine a patient and then prescribe an appropriate medicine . . . but to be a writer is more difficult . . . Medicine is something like detective work. You know that Conan Doyle who wrote *The Adventures of Sherlock Holmes* was a doctor. I read Conan Doyle first, then read medicine. The way Conan Doyle solves his problems is the way the doctor solves his cases. (Khoo, 1995, p. 297)

The Malay Dilemma, K's earliest significant work on political analysis of the day, is thus written in the mode of thinking of a doctor. As Khoo (1995) analyzed:

> Structured very much according to the methodological way that doctors approach medical problem. It will be recalled that *The Malay Dilemma* begins with a pathologist's report on what went

> wrong, on May 13, 1969 which emphasized that
> things went wrong, among other reasons, because
> 'the Government was no longer able to feel the pulse
> of the people.' The book continues with a 'history
> taking' of the influence of heredity and environment
> on the Malay race. Therefore it proceeds with a
> 'therapeutic analysis' of the Malay value system and
> code of ethics.' (p. 299)

The metaphor of doctor-politician-Sherlock Holmes is evident. Analyzing this metaphor further within the context of Malaysian society, I find that throughout his political career, K has employed a holistic approach to problem solving in the political domain. His remedies and cures for the nation involves *amputating* his political rivals he and his regime regard as cancerous, *prescribing depressants* for points of view that are not attuned to his political goals, *injecting tranquilizers* into the populace so that political reality is his and only his, *administering the strongest medicine* to political, economic, and social ills, *giving stimulants* to Malaysians so that they become good workers for the international capitalist system, and *performing plastic surgery* in areas of concern in all the spheres of Malaysian living so that they become presentable in the eyes of international audience.

Thus K, in sustaining power problem solves by administering and overseeing onto society what doctors and their variants would: hypnosis, placebo, psychoanalysis, essential vitamins, dialysis, mental therapy, physical therapy and of late, *prozac*. These are combined with traditional medicine such as those extracted from cultural arguments, religious rhetoric, and historical claims. Problem solving approaches as such, employed when he was the Prime

Minister worked well in that the nation is free from threats from organized dissenting views, feelings of political fatigue, and doubts of the government's ability to continue its onward march of state capitalism.

In continuing this writing on the facets in K's life, I now turn to a brief discussion on what guides K in his struggles or what point of view is taken in his worldview.

Facet 6: Point of View.

After briefly looking at K's epitome, central conflict, network of enterprise, ensemble of metaphors and problem-solving perspective, we now ask the question: *What guides K's point of view?*

I have argued throughout that K looks at issues as ailments to be diagnosed and issues remedies much in the manner physicians would look at them. However, in analyzing his viewpoint as a problem solving and "political imagining" individual, I extend the medical doctor-politician notion to another dimension which guides Mahathir's thinking.

The themes I will briefly illustrate will be those of "deliverance," "competition," and progress through the "catching-up game." These entail conjuring up images of "I and them," "we and they," and "us and them" in K's leit *motif* and political *modus operandi* within a *realpolitikal* paradigm characteristic of the thinking of leaders of his generation that are confronted with the challenges of liberating his people from the shackles of colonialism.

If we analyze his writings and political actions from the publication of *The Malay Dilemma* in the 1970s to his reaction to the Southeast Asian financial turmoil at the turn of this century which has bankrupt Malaysia by at least 25% of its wealth and plunge the economy into chaos, we find a pattern of K's point of view which is consistent.

The Malay Dilemma epitomizes his feelings on what went wrong with the nation and illustrates his point of view that the then, Prime Minister and his government was no longer effective in delivering the Malays out of the shackles of injustices and domination. *The Malay Dilemma* is K's point of view that he has the solution to all the ills and that the view of the government can no longer be accepted in guiding the nation. Thus, it is the "I versus them," couched in themes of deliverance, which characterized K's point of view. *The Challenge* epitomizes K's I-them characterization again, in which the enemies are the opposition parties particularly the Malaysian Islamic Party (PAS) which is considered a threat to the well being of the nation. In the publication, K again set the "I versus them" point of view in expressing his regret that these "counter-productive" forces are misguiding the people from the true path of progressive Islam and on the personal political level have almost robbed him of his necessary two-third majority in the 1986 General Elections. In his *Vision 2020* document consisting of his vision that is to be achieved by year 2020, his point of view is that of a progressive and technologically advanced Malaysia which will compete in the global arena against the advanced industrialized countries.

In all the major documents thus, the themes are those of delivering the nation from the ineffectiveness of the then government, cautioning the nation from the influences of the opposition parties, and rallying the nation to compete with advanced nations of the post-Industrial West. Justice, in K's sense of the word, consists of bringing his people out of the oppression, making them aware of their strength, sovereignty, making them work hard as good, productive, and obedient citizens, and bringing the nation to a respectable level so that Malaysia can compete and "catch up" with the world's advanced economies. In translating such a concept however, K has throughout his career employed the rhetoric of "us against them." The "them" are such as "the government of Tunku Abdul Rahman (the first Prime Minister)" the "opposition parties, "the West," "the western media," the "rogue speculators/currency traders," "European and Jews," and his other political enemies real and imagined.

Just like a traditional medicine man believes that his mystical powers is derived from his ability to communicate with forces within him, and just like a modern doctor deriving his from his training, experience and communication with his patients, K sees political power as the paramount necessity to get things done. In an interview, he spoke of power:

> I am not saying that I enjoyed power but I find that it is useful in carrying out the things you want to carry out. If you don't have power and you put out a very reasonable proposal, nobody will implement it. You have to have power. [and when asked why some people suggested that K is addictive to power and wouldn't want to let it go, K answered:] . . . it's not the question of wanting to let it go. I sense I may be wrong of course, that people do not want me to go just yet. They keep on telling me that. Of course they may be sycophants. But the fact is that they say that what I am doing has made the country what it is today. Well, they say, I may be wrong, they may be wrong. (Mitton, 1997, pp.12-13)

To K, power has brought him achievements in his 22-year rule. When asked if he had been in power too long, he replied:

> People will think it is too long. But one thing you can be sure of is that the certainty of your demise will undermine your ability to run the country. The problem with many countries is that their leaders are only allowed to do one term. People don't respect that one term because you are going to go out anyway. (Mitton, 1997, p. 9)

Thus, from K's point of view, power to make changes to the nation and to solve problems comes from one's clinging onto it and also from one's ability to believe that he will continue to reign "as long as the people need him." Such point of view, is characteristic of many a Third World leader political demagogue. Names like Mohamed Suharto of Indonesia (32 years), Lee Kuan Yew of Singapore (20 years and who is at present a Senior Minister), Ferdinand Marcos of the Philippines (20 years) and Fidel Castro of Cuba (more than 20 years) are among those who can be analyzed as having similar points of view concerning the passion for total power.

From K's point of view, "creativity" and problem solving in the political domain can be exercised if one has the power to eliminate all barriers by any means necessary in order for his agenda to be successfully carried out. These creativity and problem-solving methods include variants of xenophobia, creating "enemies" for the nation to rally against, enhancing his public image using the state-controlled media, and looking for scapegoats such as the "West," "Western media," "Jewish conspiracy," and "George Soros" to cover up his shortcomings. His view on his "frankness" and "directness" (clearly a "Western" trait) however is trumpeted, illustrated in the *Asiaweek* interview in which he spoke against the label "ultra-Malay" he has been characterized as:

> I was never an ultra. That was a label given to me because I tended to speak my mind. I called a spade a spade, as they say. So one way to negate the effect of anybody is to label him as being slightly off center. A little bit mad. That way, anything that he says will be treated as coming from a mad man or an ultra. I was never an ultra. I was just willing to speak my mind. Even now I'm still saying it. I never minced words. If I find something wrong, I'll say it, whether it is with regard to the Malays or with regard to the Chinese or with regard to other countries—big or small—I just speak my mind. I think that things need to be said and I'll say it. (Mitton, 1997, p. 9)

It is ironic then that those arrested for their strong view points—on religious freedom, on environmental degradation, on more accountable democracy—who called "a spade a spade" but do not have the power K has can be arrested and detained without trial for a maximum of two years.

Whatever the irony is, K's perspectives prevails; one that has guided him in his problem solving and creativity approaches. To him, his opinions are absolute, more than those of collective decision of the judiciary of which he has silenced over the last many years since he was given power by those who voted. An interesting example of how K maintained his point of view throughout his career can be illustrated by a comment made by a former Lord President as he compares K with the Prime Ministers (Tunku, Razak, and Hussein) before him:

> Hussein Onn, after his retirement, said that the greatest mistake I ever made was to make Mahathir my deputy . . . And the Tunku said many times that we have a diabolical PM [Prime Minister]; he is autocratic . . . you have to agree with Mahathir on everything or he'll try to destroy you. But with the Tunku, Razak, and Hussein, you could disagree with them and they still asked you home to dinner. (Mitton, 1997, p. 4)

For K thus, power is to be used to the maximum in consolidating his position so that he can continue to create and solve problems.

Facet 7: Development.

In discussing K's creativity and problem solving approaches, it can be said that their development follows a topographical pattern of communitarianistic thinking. Consistent with my previous analysis of K's point of view characteristic of the "us versus them" thinking, it can be said that K's early work, *The Malay Dilemma* argues for equal economic participation for the Malays against the non-Malays (the Chinese particularly) so that the indigenous people can have its 30 % ownership of the nation's economic pie. The Malays are to be taken out of their inferior economic status of merely being agricultural producers and through education, economic participation, and rapid urbanization be lifted out of the injustices that was created by the British colonials.

Such was his analysis of the root of inequality; the need for urbanization and to restructure the economy based along communal lines in order to affect the necessary changes for his people (Mohamad, 1970). Upon assuming work as Minister of Education, K translated such communitarian view with policies which would ensure that the Malays for example gain 30% participation in universities so that the "professional class" of Malays would later be created. Not only K advocated and implemented policies towards redressing the racial imbalances but also called for a "mental revolution" in the Malays and the non-Malays; the former are to be ready for changes for a McClelland—type of modernization drive and the latter are to accept the affirmative action programs to be implemented. Thus, through the New Economic Policies drawn up every five years, starting from 1970, racial inequality in terms of income distribution and membership of wealth became the centerpiece of Malaysia's strategic planning. Communitarian thinking within the milieu of communal politics became the guiding force of K's development as a problem-solver.

Whilst in *The Malay Dilemma*, K's thinking is based along that of Malay nationalism and the need to create a professional class of Malay urbanites, in *The Challenge*, K's rhetoric and policy analysis moved towards Islamic-based arguments. As noted in earlier sections, *The Challenge* is a writing on ideas documented in the midst of the growing pressure on the government to Islamize Malaysia and particularly to counter the pressure from the Malaysian Islamic party (Pan Islamic Malaysian Party) which was growing more popular with the rural and urban Malays. K attacked parties based on socialist principles; the Democratic Action Party, and the Malaysian Socialist Party—these two together with the Malaysian Islamic party formed a coalition known as the *"Angkatan Perpaduan Ummah"* (The Brigade of People's Unity) and almost robbed K's ruling coalition of its needed two-thirds majority.

K's development as a thinker thus moved from a Malay-centric communitarian to a "syncretist of convenience" who warned people against Western-styled capitalism and socialism (and Communism) and advocated Islamic form of economic thinking. In his opening chapter of "The Poor are Poorer, the Rich, Richer!" the following excerpts illustrate K's development of such syncretist perspective:

> In recent times, the ideology and logic of materialism have all too easily influenced human society. This is the direct result of the impact of Western thought and system of values, which fanatically focuses in the material as the basis of life. Values based on the spiritual, on the peace of mind, and on the belief in feelings loftier than desire, have no place in Western psyche ... Based on these materialistic concepts and values, a slogan has been concocted to influence the minds and hearts of the people. It goes: 'The poor are poorer, the rich, richer!' Created by socialists in the West, the slogan has spread and infected the rest of the world. Among the communities caught in its trap are the Malays of Malaysia. (Mohamad, 1986, p. 4)

It is to be noted that towards the late 1980s at the time K has translated most of his ideas set forth in *The*

Malay Dilemma, the government's policies created several millionaires among the Malays whose role models are American capitalists such as the Vanderbilts, the Rockefellers, the Du Ponts and the Carnegies. In buffering the criticisms that the Malaysian rich are getting richer, K thus advocated an Islamic version of capitalistic and socialistic thinking. K quoted Islamic conception of justice in wealth distribution:

> The history of Islam clearly shows that its followers practice moderation in all their dealings. Wealth is not disapproved of and certainly not forbidden. What Islam wants is that the rich help the poor voluntarily through alms and also through the payment of the religious tithes, *zakat* and *fitrah*. In this way society is not faced with the problem of excessive imbalance . . . Since the payment of the *zakat* is one of the duties of the rich, they cannot feel proud about it or consider the poor indebted to them. But if they give alms, i.e. over and above what is compulsory, their kindness will certainly be appreciated by society. This will further improve the social climate and make for an even more peaceful and happy society. (Mohamad, 1986, p. 15)

Thus K rejects American styled—capitalism and the then Soviet Union—styled socialism *in toto* as, according to him, they are both based upon materialism. He advocated a mixed economy based upon Islamic principles. Throughout his development as a creative and problem-solving individual, he consistently used this *leitmotif* to maintain power. Exactly where the rhetoric and reality is demarcated in his thinking is not known albeit many a writing critical of the government's development policies have pointed out to the fact that Malaysia still remains a Third World country producing for the global capitalist market. The turmoil in Southeast Asian economy however pointed out clearly the infallibility of such an economic system which is vulnerable to any Domino effect of the fall of Asian capitalism.

K's thinking along communitarian ideals continue to be developed in his conception of Malaysia as a fully industrialized state by January 1, 2020. In his document *Vision 2020* K outlined challenges the nation needs to meet in order to become competitive in the global market. His communitarianism lies in his belief that not only Malaysia needs to compete as an economic grouping to compete with existing trade blocks such as the Asian Free Trade Area (AFTA), North Atlantic Free Trade Area (NAFTA) Asia Pacific Economic Conference (APEC) and the European Economic Community (EEC, now European Union, or the EU). His vision for East Asia Economic Caucus (EAEC) although announced in 1990, is still waiting to be realized as the proposed members of the caucus felt that the proposal is only to give Malaysia the greatest advantage.

Throughout his 22—year rule, K's creative development did not change in the sense that communitarianism, rather than cosmopolitanism in thinking remained. His central conflict of rallying "us against them" remains his guiding principle although creative ideas of magnitude have indeed been produced. Creativity and problem-solving approaches are to be employed from his point of view predominantly and that what he produces is novel, of purpose, of value, and within a certain time frame insofar as they come out of his mould. During the economic quagmire brought about by the 1997 Asian Financial crisis, K is still insistent that the country does not need to include members of the opposition party to advise the government what steps needed to be taken in order to save the nation from total economic chaos. Nor does K wanted international agencies such as the International Monetary Fund to bail Malaysia out. Hence, K's creative development revolves around communitarianism in political will and actions.

Facet 8: Interpretive work.

In looking at the last facet, interpretive work in this study of Mahathir Mohamad as a creative problem solver in the political domain, I have chosen to analyze the central idea of *Vision 2020*, a document which was originally written as a speech by K to the Malaysian Business Council and delivered on 28 February 1991. *Vision 2020* can be said to be one of the culminations of K's work throughout his career as a Prime Minister. It charted the challenges the nation need to face in order for it to develop at par with the advanced nations of the world. K outlined nine challenges summarized below:

> *The first* of these is the challenge of establishing a united Malaysian nation with a sense of common and shared destiny . . .
>
> *The second* is the challenge of creating a psychologically liberated, secure, and developed Malaysian society with faith and confidence in itself, justifiably proud of what it is, of what it has accomplished, robust enough to face all manner of adversity . . .
>
> *The third* challenge . . . is that of fostering and developing a mature democratic society, practicing a form of mature consensual, community-oriented

Malaysian democracy that can be a model for many developing countries . . .

The fourth challenge is establishing a fully moral and ethical society whose citizens are strong in religious and spiritual values and with the highest ethical standard . . .

The fifth challenge . . . is the challenge of establishing a matured, liberal and tolerant society in which Malaysians of all colors and creed are free to practice and profess their customs, cultures and religious beliefs and yet feeling that they belong to one nation . . .

The sixth challenge is the challenge of establishing a scientific and progressive society, a society that is innovative and forward-looking, one that is not only a consumer of technology but also a contributor to the scientific and technological civilization of the future . . .

The seventh challenge is the challenge of establishing a fully caring society and caring culture, a social system in which society will come before the self, in which welfare of the people will revolve not around the state or the individual but around a strong and resilient family system.

The eighth is the challenge of ensuring an economically just society . . . in which there is a fair and equitable distribution of the wealth of the nation, in which there is full partnership in economic progress . . .

[And lastly] *the ninth* challenge is the challenge of establishing a prosperous society with an economy that is fully competitive, dynamic, robust and resilient. (Mohamad, 1991, pp. 2–3; emphases added)

Throughout the document, K elaborated the *modus operandi* for the nation to be fully industrialized *via* its own mould with the full participation of every citizen, government agency and the private sector.

Vision 2020 is a document which would help the nation achieve the status of a fully developed nation by January 1, 2020. In it contains statements of hope; presents all the ingredients needed for a multiracial, capitalistic and nationalistic society to progress. It reflects K's philosophy of governing and contains themes, which are continuations of what have been said by other prime ministers since the country gained independence. *Vision 2020* illustrates K's vision as a futurist and strategic thinker and also his never-ending insistence to accelerate the nation's development process so that Malaysia can compete in the world system. If we examine it for its meaning we would note that K's vision document, a creative product based on principles of problem solving have its novelty, purpose, value and duration. The novelty of it is in its strategic plan for the twenty-first century, the purpose is to guide the nation towards full industrialization, the value is in its utilitarianism for K's society and lastly the duration is K's cumulative work for the nation to achieve the goals by the year 2020.

The document in addition, is also a testament of K's and his government's commitment to free enterprise and capitalism couched in cultural and religious terms. As in K's argument in *The Challenge* in which he attempted to denounce "godless" capitalism and socialism, *Vision 2020* attempts to achieve a similar effect. It attempts to harness the continuing support of the people by drawing out plans which would be acceptable to even the opposition parties. The idea of capitalism with rural and religious bases, economic development with inevitable trickle-down effect, social maturity with democracy and liberalism—all these are propagated well enough "to the year 2020!" In fact, the term Vision 2020 is a metaphor for a continuing state of being for the nation to have a clear view; a "20/20 Vision" in an eye doctor's language, so that K's government will have a "rain check" beyond the year 2000.

Analyzing the document in further detail, we may also find that it is written in a language of "competition and combat," of getting ready to go to war with the economic superpowers of the world, and of preparing the nation spiritually and religiously before the war. Although Malaysia is a historically peaceful nation, which only in its post-Independence history has had to fight against Indonesia's aggression in 1965, the document does reflect economic militaristic tendencies. Khoo (1995) observed:

> The language of contest and preparation for combat is not derived from any militaristic tradition in Malaysian politics; there is none. But it is fitting that Vision 2020, the ideological expression of Mahathir's 'mature' nationalism, should be so permeated with capitalism's idiom of combat and contest. Within this scenario of trade wars and struggles for market shares, Vision 2020 specifies that its 'first strategic challenge' lies in 'establishing a united Malaysian nation' possessed of a 'sense of common and shared destiny,' shored up by a 'full and fair partnership' and made up by one '*Bangsa Malaysia*' or 'Malaysian race.' (pp. 330-331)

To K, the meaning of the document lies in his ability to draw up such a plan as a testament of his ability to still maintain power after all those years. It also reflects his achievement in bringing the nation through successive stages of industrialization much of what he envisioned in his early work *The Malay Dilemma*. K wrote in the document:

> We have already come a long way towards the fulfillment of these objectives [challenges of Vision 2020]. The nine central objectives need not be our order of priorities over the next three decades. Most obviously, the priorities of any moment in time must meet the specific circumstances of that moment in time. (p. 3)

The above statement is ambiguous if we analyze the document as a goal to be met by January 1, 2020. But if we look at K's vision of a developed nation as one of a process of "being and becoming" we may find that what is meant is that there will be sectors in the Malaysian economy, predominantly the corporate, which have already achieved the objectives. These are the ones which have accumulated wealth internationally and whose workers get paid two to three times higher than those in the government sector.

The above questions are but a few critical questions relating to K's *Vision 2020*. Nonetheless, the document illustrates further K's maturity in translating his actual conflict as I have discussed at length in previous sections. In *The Malay Dilemma*, the conflict is to liberate the Malays from the non-Malays and the then government, in *The Challenge*, it is to warn the electorate from political parties adverse to K's coalition government and in *Vision 2020*, it is to prepare a liberated Malaysia for competition in the aggressive global market.

The document is thus K's interpretive work on what he constitute as his epitome as a glorified state leader who will continue to bring his people into the twenty-first century with the confidence that his government will continue to rule beyond January 1, 2020. And out of the idea in *The Challenge* came *Vision 2020* and its physical manifestation: The Multimedia Super Corridor. Figure 15 below illustrates the relationship between Mahathir's *Vision 2020* and The Multimedia Super corridor. While the philosophy guides the idea of hypermodernity of a metaphysical journey of social advancement, it is also a meaningless catchphrase.

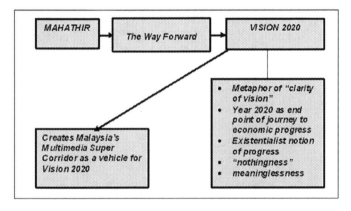

Figure 15: Mahathir's Vision 2020

Thus in brief, this analysis of K's work can be said to be a testament of his ability to state with confidence that as long as the country is under his rule, he will decide what shape it will take and which way forward it will follow; through a mature political system that evolved form politics of consensus to hegemony or the production of a certain form of consciousness one may call "Mahathirism" (Hilley, 2001; Khoo, 1995).

Portrait of Mahathir as an Evolving System

From the information on K's eight facets analyzed above, I now discuss the semantic portrait of Malaysia's fourth prime minister to understand how he has maintained power for more than 22 years. As Figure 16 below suggests, the author of the MSC, having had the privilege of being in power that long, creates new systems of thinking about economic, social, and political development. From the Figure below, one can see the semantic relationship of ideas around the author: creation, destruction, sustenance, and containment. For instance, the map of inter-texts of the individual illustrate how authoritarianism operates such that the developmentalist agenda necessitates the emergence of a leader that uses power to the fullest extent to author inscriptions and installations and to advance ideology with the use of the state's ideological apparatuses.

In the final analysis, as Figure 17 below suggests, the author directs the nation through his authorship (the national development policies,) creates strong philosophy of authoritarianism, establishes autocratic rule, and finally creates automatons out of those he governed. The ideological state apparatus is used to command and control and to help him and his regime achieve the ends of subjugation. This situation is a classic example of hyper-modern colonial rule exemplified and inspired by the British system of colonial administration.

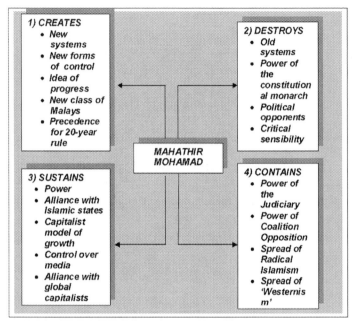

Figure 16: Semantic Portrait of Mahathir as Intertext

It is through this Asian–Machiavellian style of leadership that the author inscribes fear and structure obedience into the minds of those he rules; and nurtures the growth of hegemonic conditions. As explained in the figure below, Mahathir Mohamad's authorship of the Multimedia Super Corridor as well as the national agenda for progress creates in the long run, a better form of authoritarianism which then evolve into the style of autocratic rule which consequently produces "automatons" out of the thinking of the people that are governed.

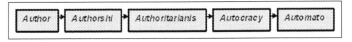

Figure 17: In the Hands of the Author

Conclusion

In analyzing the mind of Malaysia's fourth Prime Minister, a medical doctor—turned politician, a political survivor, and author of the MSC, I have attempted to use Gruber's Evolving Systems Approach (1989) in looking at the subject as a case study of a creative thinker and problem solver. The facets outlined are but brief illustrations of the mind of an individual who has used political imagination to maintain power and use it in the manner he desires. Creativity in the political and moral domain, that is, to bring about novel changes to bring out people out of the shackles of mental domination has been the thrust of my discussions. Essentially the desire to maintain power whilst to bring the nation through seemingly moral and intellectual leadership is what constitutes hegemony.

In the next chapter, I discuss the artifact the author creates and the subject of inquiry on hegemonic formations: The Malaysian Multimedia Super Corridor (The MSC). I will discuss the origin of it as well as of the mantra of the "Information Age" used as a source of inspiration for Malaysia's cybernetic transformation.

Chapter VI

THE MANTRA AND ITS ORIGIN: APPROPRIATION OF IDEOLOGY

"He has erected a multitude of New Offices, and sent hither swarms of Officers to harass our people, and eat out their substance"

—From *Representatives of the United States of America. Declaration of Independence* (Jefferson,1776/2003)

Cyberjaya and Malaysia's Multimedia Super Corridor (MSC) Project

In the preceding chapter, using the eight facets of The Evolving Systems Approach, I discussed the thought-process of Malaysia's fourth and longest-serving prime minister, Mahathir Mohamad, retired from power after more than twenty two years, i.e. fourteen years more than any American president can be in office. Mahathir was able to author the nation into one that appears conditioned to fear the State and its policing apparatuses. The Internal Security Act (ISA) is used to intimidate, investigate, imprison without trial those who oppose the ruling government. The ideological state apparatuses is used by the regime to maintain power and, styled after British colonialism, to divide and rule. In the previous chapter too I discussed how the idea of authoritarianism was developed to develop a nationhood that is characteristic of a polity in a state of automaton. I discussed at length Mahathir's artifact or his regime's authorship called *Vision 2020* that charts the nation's developmentalist agenda to the year, albeit metaphorical, 2020. Out of the document emanate the real estate venture called The Multimedia Super Corridor (MSC). I discuss below the origin of the project.

Under Mahathir, Malaysia created what is called a "cyber-society" run from an administrative capital called *Putrajaya* located in its grand scale project, The MSC. The latter is built on several hundred square kilometers of area in which "seven flagship applications" is its feature. It mimics California's Silicon Valley and models after what Castells and Hall (1994) call the concept of a "technopole" by which Malaysia (see Figure 18) will be moved to a new paradigm of living based upon the "humane application of high technology" manifested in the sub concepts of Electronic Government, Electronic Banking, Electronic Commerce, Manufacturing, Research and Development, Smart Cards, and National Smart Schools. Interestingly, the word "application" as commonly used to describe a computer program is used in the Malaysian MSC project as a major sector of the economy to be transformed on a grand scale.

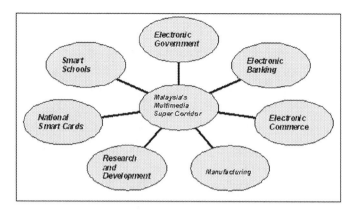

Figure 18: The Flagship Applications of the Malaysian Multimedia Super Corridor

The biggest airport in Asia, the Kuala Lumpur International Airport was built to facilitate the development of *Cyberjaya*. From the "wired-up" capital city as the initial program of mega-structural change, the Malaysian government planned to create cyber-principalities out of the thirteen states constituting the federation.

Mahathir envisioned that by the metaphorical year of 2020, the country will have achieved in its own mould the status of an advanced fully-industrialized nation able to compete with other advanced industrialized economies namely the United States of America, Europe, Japan, and Singapore. Accordingly, the notion of such an advancement would however be based upon a strong foundation of religious and moral values. The Prime Minister eulogizes in "Cyberjaya: The model intelligent city in the making":

Cyberjaya is envisaged to be the model multimedia haven for leading, innovative multimedia companies from all over the world to spin a 'web' that will mutually enrich all those involved with it. Especially created as the first MSC designated cybercity, it enables world-class companies to take full advantage of the unique package Malaysia offers to create an environment that is fully conducive towards exacerbating the growth of information technology and multimedia industries. It offers a high capacity global and logistics infrastructure, backed by a 'soft' infrastructure, which includes financial incentives and competitive telecoms tariffs, as well as a set of new cyberlaws that will form a legal framework to facilitate the growth of electronic commerce. (Mohamad, MDC, n.d., p. 2)

Malaysia—Co-authored by International Inscribers

In realizing this dream, Malaysia invited a panel of advisors from the United States, Europe, and Japan, among these Chief Executive Officers/Presidents of corporations such as Acer Incorporated, Alcatel Alsthom, Microsoft Corporation, Bechtel Group Incorporated, British Telecom, Cisco Systems, Compaq Computers Corporation, DHL, Ericsson, Fujitsu Limited, Hewlett Packard, IBM, Motorola Corporation, Netscape Communications, Reuters, Motion Picture Association of America, Twentieth Century Fox, Bloomberg and tens of others of global giants in the telematics and media-related industries. Mahathir chairs the panel whereas the respective companies set up shop in the technological growth area.

Professors of Business and Public Policy from Silicon Valley's Stanford University are among those guiding the development of Malaysia's cyber initiatives. Malaysian subsidiaries of these giants in the world of multi-billion dollar club transnational corporations have been set up for such a project. There are also active "world-class" companies in operation in the MSC. Table 1 below summarizes information on some of the world-class companies/international inscribers of Malaysia's project.

The experience of the technological industry in California became an impetus and hence a text to be translated in the case of the creation of Malaysia's MSC. The role of the International Advisory Panel as corporate authors can be a good illustration of how under the regime of Mahathir, the state continues to be authored by foreign writers in the guise of an International Advisory Panel to the Multimedia Super Corridor. As of September 2003, there is a total of 149 members of the advisory panel.

The advisory panel meets every year to primarily give advice on strategic matters of the nation's transformation as well as to give the image that Malaysia's development is in harmony with the well-being of the world's giant transnational corporations.

Table 1: International Co-authors of the MSC

COMPANY	COUNTRY OF ORIGIN
NTT	Japan
Intel	USA
Siemens Multimedia	Germany
Fujitsu	Japan
DHL	U.S.A
Motorola Multimedia	U.S.A
Fujitsu Telecoms	Japan
Sun Microsystems	U.S.A
BT Multimedia	Netherlands
Lucent Technologies	U.S.A.
S.I.T.A. (Societe Internationale De Telecommunications Aeronautiques)	Belgium
Nokia	Finland
EDS	U.S.A
Unisys	U.S.A
Reuters	U.K
Bloomberg	U.S.A
Ericsson	Sweden
Microsoft	U.S.A.
Rockwell Automation	Singapore/Malaysia
Shell Information Technology	Holland
British American Tobacco	Britain, U.S.A
Castlewood System	U.S.A
Alcatel Networks	France
Reach Internet Services	Hong Kong/Australia

IBM	U.S.A.
Comptel Communications	Finland
Lotus Engineering	United Kingdom
Technomen	Finland
Biodata Systems	Germany
Scope International	United Kingdom
CISCO	U.S.A
Huawei Technologies	Hong Kong
Fortum Sendi	United Kingdom
IT-365 Malaysia	United Kingdom
Satyam Computer Services	India
Smart Trust	Finland
AVEVA	United Kingdom
SAP Learning Technologies	Singapore
Shell Global Solutions	Netherlands
Schlumberger Technologies	France
HSBC Electronic Data Processing	United Kingdom
NEC Systems Integration	Japan
WIPRO Limited	India
BMW Technology	Germany
Computer Associates	U.S.A.

Figure 19 below suggests the genealogy of the MSC. The experience of California's Silicon Valley, in which the growth area of the Orange County is aided by the scientific and technological innovative activities of Stanford University, is appropriated in the case of the creation of the MSC. The idea of transforming the nation perhaps existed before the creation of Malaysia's National Informational

Technology Council. Next, came the creation of the Multimedia Development Corporation that oversees the development of The Malaysian Multimedia Super Corridor.

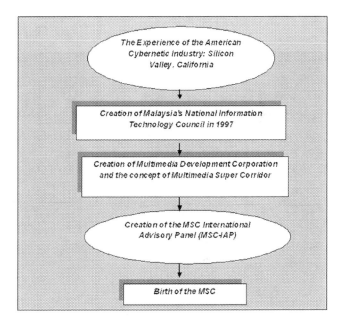

Figure 19: The History of the MSC

Conclusion

The economic growth experience of an advanced nation such as The United States of America and especially in the case of the growth of the Silicon Valley became an inspiration for Malaysia's program of national development. While in the case of Stanford University and Orange County California the growth seem natural, arising out of the technological culture that was nurtured through decades of research and development, Malaysia took the initiative of copying the model and downloading the concept to engineer a program of immediate inscription and installation of the ideology of information-based economic growth. The mentorship for this program of hypermodernized transformation comes from the conglomerate of corporate capitalist of the advanced developing world, most obviously form global-reaching and imperialistic companies such as Microsoft, Netscape, Sony, British Telecom, and even Bloomberg and The Motion Picture Association of America. The mantra of informational technology that has its origin in the research labs at Palo Alto California hence is chanted in Malaysia and the chants inscribed onto the landscape through the authoritarianism of its leader. In the next chapter, I discuss in detail how the mantra that became policies and ideology become texts in corporate brochures, ready to be broadcast and disseminated to the international and local corporate investor and to the *rakyat* (people) of Malaysia.

PART 3

INSCRIPTION OF IDEOLOGY

Chapter VII

INSCRIPTION #1: ANALYSIS OF SELECT BROCHURES

"The presence of MMU [the Multimedia University,], Tenaga University and Universiti Putra Malaysia will seek to emulate the Stanford—inspired setting of Silicon Valley and create a networked, creative and productive society in Cyberjaya."

— Mahathir Mohamad

Introduction

In this first analytical chapter, I begin by analyzing the first set of inscriptions i.e., brochures of the institutions installed onto the MSC. Select visuals from the brochure, "Malaysia in the new millennium" (MDC Corporate Affairs Department, n.d.) are analyzed. Another major analysis are a two-page visuals from a brochure on the new administrative capital of Putrajaya. To further strengthen this first exercise in the series of analysis of inscriptions, I also write about the sign, signifier, and signified from three supporting visuals. They are select pages of brochures

121

relating to Malaysia's Multimedia Super Corridor entitled: "Unlocking the potentials of the information age" (MDC, 1997), "Cyberjaya: The model intelligent city in the making" (MDC, n.d.), and "Putrajaya: The federal government administrative center" (Putrajaya Holdings, 1997).

Framework of Analysis

Rose (2001) described the method of semiotics in analyzing claims produced in advertisements. Rose discussed two forms of discourse analyses (I and II) which looks at texts (verbal and visual) and attempt to uncover the dimensions of power and ideology behind the production of these texts. In analyzing images from the brochures, I utilize the guiding questions provided by Rose to analyze the images of The Multimedia Super Corridor, Cyberjaya, and Putrajaya. I look at the general display of images, the placement of the texts, the signs and symbols, and the overt and covert displays, and the perceived message intended to be communicated.

Visual #1, Figure #20

In the first visual, I entitled "Machines in the Garden" (Figure 20 below), the logo of the MSC is placed on the upper left-hand side, lower left-hand side, and lower right-hand side of the brochure. The biggest of the logo is the first one mentioned above. The first paragraph of the text on the left reads "Our logo is based on the concept of a rising sun, signifying the dawning of a new era in Malaysia to be ushered in with the Multimedia Super Corridor (MSC)" (MDC Corporate Affairs Department, n.d., p.1) The idea of a rising sun is reminiscent of the days of Japanese imperialism in Southeast Asia[15] and in the time of the regime of Mahathir, the "Look East Policy," promotes the spirit of borrowing from the East rather than bowing to the West. The Multimedia Super Corridor becomes the vehicle of structural changes.

I call the composite picture "Machines in the garden," a title inspired by a piece of work eulogizing the transformation of pastoral America (Marx, 1964/2000). I find the positioning of the collection of composite images interesting. From the image of a Malay executive staring at a computer screen to a satellite disc in the foreground of a lush tropical landscape, one can interpret the signs, symbols, and signifiers from the levels of the grammar of design to the level of analysis of power and ideology.

---

[15] During the "Japanese Interregnum," Malaya was a colony of Japan. The rise of Malay nationalism was said to be a consequence of the victory of the Japanese (a member of the Germany-Italian-Japanese Axis powers of World War II) in becoming the new colonizers and imperialists in Southeast Asia.

Figure 20: Machines in the Garden, Visual #1

By grammar of design, I mean the layout of the picture to render the images effective to the reader. A right-handed person would begin by focusing on the right hand side and be introduced to the image of hypermodernity. One's gaze might even stop at the symbol of Apple Computer propped between the image of the thinking executive and the satellite disc. In the background is a lush tropical landscape. Among other images is the image of students working at a computer lab.

By the analysis of power and ideology, I mean the idea that in general, the images signify the power inherent in telecommunications and computer technology in particular, signify a promoter of radical and intensified social change as well as an agent of change in the relations of production. By ideology, I mean the idea of a vision of that social change carved and crafted out of cybernetics technology. At the level of the grammar of design, I see the motive of the producer of the text influencing the reader to believe in the changes that are happening as advertised. By power and ideology, I mean the inevitable march of progress *via* the philosophy of technological determinism.

In Table 2 below, I draw the semiotic elements of the MSC logo. The Rising Sun signified the dawning of a new era. The three rays for example, signify high capacity global telecommunications and logistic infrastructure whereas the heart of the logo signifies environmental considerations. The arch, on the other hand, represents unity of forces shaping the new era of change.

Table 2: Semiotic Analysis of the MSC Logo

SIGN	SIGNIFIER	SIGNIFIED
Logo	Rising sun	Dawning of a new era
	Three rays	1. High capacity global telecommunications and logistics infrastructure 2. New Policies and cyberlaws 3. Attractive environment to live in
	Heart of the logo	Environmental consideration
	Arch	Unification of diverse strengths; pre-requisite for success

In Table 3, I draw semiotic elements of the composite images. Among them are: the landscape/rolling hills in the picture signifies harmony and suggests that Nature is to be transformed and conquered by hyper-miniaturized or nano technology as a consequence of the demands of globalization and the dictates of corporate capitalism. The Malaysian economic landscape is also transformed by the movement of money or the globalization of finance,

125

in addition to the globalization of ideas, people, and technology (see Appadurai, 1996). The Satellite dish is a signifier for communication which signifies globalization. The computer is the tool par excellence that facilitates progress. It is an advertisement that signifies corporate capitalism. The image of students in a computer lab, is one that signifies the computerization of human beings through the process of schooling as social reproduction; a process tied to the international economic system (see Ashton & Greene, 1996).

Table 3: Semiotic Analysis of Machines in the Garden

SIGN	SIGNIFIER	SIGNIFIED
Landscape/Rolling hills	Harmonizing	Nature
Huge Satellite dish	Communicating	Globalization
APPLE computer	Advertising	Corporate capitalism
Students at computer lab	One-dimensionalizing	Computerization of humans
Laptop computer	minimizing/ transporting	Nano-technology
ATM screen	Storing and retrieving	Finance
Computer headphones	Individualizing	One-dimensionalization

The essence of the idea of transformation lies in the notion of the implantation of ideology and the inscribing of real estate onto the landscape of Malaysia; that institutions were set up to give expression to changes that are based on a well-directed strategy of national development. As read from the visual, the impact of the social and cultural changes lies in the education as a vehicle of change; to create the "one-dimensionalization" of individuals through a process commonly called human engineering and manpower planning. Malaysia, in the new millennium signifies not only the idea of progress based on the supremacy of the philosophy of cybernetics as a deterministic force but also the molding of the polity and the populace into computer-literate beings that will act, think, feel, and speak using the jargons of "computerese." Malaysia in the new millennium is a transformed Malaysia; from agricultural to manufacturing, to more sophisticated manufacturing. The stages of growth nonetheless is frameworked after Rostowian and Friedmannian economics or, ideology of capitalism with a tinge of nationalism.

Visual #2, Figure 21

In Figure 21 below, which I entitled, "Inside the machines in the garden," are images such as a map of the MSC presented as a highlighted area in the Southeast Asia region, a "Please Click" icon, the Earth, a picture of the lobby of the headquarters of the Multimedia Development Corporation in Cyberjaya, fibre optics, a man sitting in front of a laptop computer and five people gathering in front of a computer (headed by a Caucasian male 'mentoring' an Asian woman). There is also an arch on the top left-hand corner of the page with little icons superimposed on it. Among them are of an eye, a telephone, a floppy disk, a television monitor, and a satellite dish. All these images appear on the top right and left hand corner of the text on the page. The titles and sub-titles on the page are: "What is the Multimedia Super Corridor?," "What makes the

MSC special?," and "Who overseas what goes on within the MSC?."

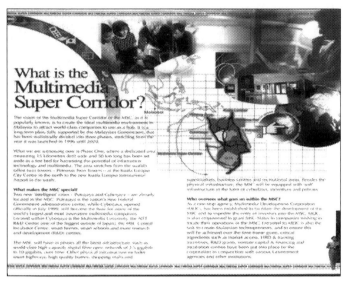

Figure 21: Inside the Machines in the Garden, Visual #2

In Table 4 I provide a summary of the important themes. For example, a "map" would signify a new territory. And "people gathering/meeting" would signify the activities of a corporation (making decisions, solving problems, designing strategies, and so on). The activities are driven by computer technology; the relations of ideological and social production are managed by digital communications. The image on the left-hand corner of the page of the arch with little icons, signify communication technologies that are transforming the country. The image suggests technological determinism as a driving force of Malaysia's economic development. The man with the laptop computer is emblematic of the image of the mobility of the modern corporate executive; that capitalism itself necessitates the movement of not only money, products, ideas, and services, but also people. The corporate executive seems free to move but yet shackled by the technology that helps those who owns capital chase him/her around the globe.

Table 4: Semiotic Analysis of the Introduction to MSC

SIGN	SIGNIFIER	SIGNIFIED
Map	Charting and colonizing	New territory
Hand clicking	Automating	Control
Lobby	Arriving/Waiting/Departing	Transit
Laptop	Minimizing/transporting/mobility	Nano-technology
People gathering/meeting	Decision making, problem solving, and so on	Activities of a Corporation
Icons on the arch	Communication technology	Technological determinism

Visual #3, Figure 22

Figure 22 below is my analysis of the next image from the same brochure above. In it I see the sign and symbols of education as social reproduction in the form of what looked like students busy doing classwork in a computer lab. I interpret the image of school computer (sign) lab as the transformation of the classroom (signifier) in the new practice of "education as social reproduction" (signified). The image shown is clearly that of Apple Computers. Specifically, the picture on the right hand side is that of *Apple's iMAC* computer. Most of the children in this picture are Malaysian Chinese. Malaysian Malays and 'Bumiputras' represent 55% of the population. The image of individualized learning with each student having access to one computer is a representation of the ideal. Above the image is that of a corporate executive with a laptop. This is the image of what the children are to aspire to become.

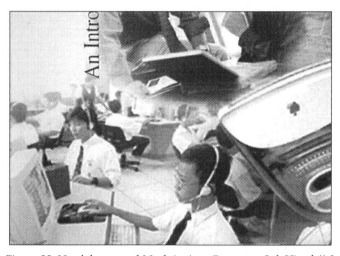

Figure 22: Headphones and Neckties in a Computer Lab, Visual # 3
(*Evolving a Culture of Managerial and Therapeutic Individualism*)

Out of the 10,000 schools promised to be equipped with computers by the year 2010, about a hundred were designated as "Smart Schools". There is a question of equity and the phenomena of "showcase-ness" in this project. The composite image also consists of one that represents the image of Malaysia's future. Whilst the students represent the immediate future of technologizing education, the image of a group of people looking at the screen of a laptop computer. Represented is the image of preparation of junior members of the society (see Dewey, 1997) to become citizens in a global capitalist world (see Carnoy & Levin, 1985.) Represented in the signs, symbols, and signifiers of the composite image is the notion of reproduction of the members of the society, through education for efficiency and productivity, into the managerial class that labors locally and globally and whose labor, in this new world economy is appropriated by international capitalists (see Freire, 1986; McLaren; 1997; Willis, 1977). The title of the visual "Neckties and Headphones in a Computer Lab" explains the idea of Malaysia's program of creating a managerial class which Bellah, Madsen, Sullivan, Swidler, and Tipton (1985) might call individualists that will embody the individualism of America's managerial class. Through the creation of this class then the individualism of the "therapeutic" nature will evolve. The notion of managers a rational, efficient, calculative, systematic, thinks like cogs in the wheels of global capitalism, is juxtaposed with the idea of the individual, after having their emotions fragmented and quantified, needs therapy payable at hourly rates. Perhaps this is not the vision of society desired by Mahathir, but the development of the modern corporate-capitalist state modeled after the United States may dictate social development as such.

Visual #4, Figure 23

The image below (Visual #4, Figure 23) is one of Malaysian progress. In it are signs, symbols and signifiers of the new Malaysia that has evolved out of the interplay between nationalism, technology, culture, and globalization.

A young woman of Indian descent sits in front of a neatly-arranged set of encyclopedia in a library, emblematic of the image of one studying for a law or a medical degree. Indians and those of South and North Indian descent are portrayed here as aspiring lawyers or perhaps medical doctors. Malays are portrayed as the preserver of the Malay tradition and in this case, specifically as traditional dancers that skillful in the art of entertaining tourists.

The image signifies the Malays as traditional entertainers for the Malay Sultan, always abidingly ready to please the traditional monarchs. This perhaps befits the new image of the city of Putrajaya, one whose name is derived by the son of the Sultan of Kedah who became, with the blessing of the outgoing British colonial masters, Malaysia's first Prime Minister. In the modern age wherein tourism is a major economic activity for Malaysia, the dance troupes play an important role in the cultural-industrial complex. In the page of the brochure there is also, an image of a baseball stadium, although baseball is not a popular game at all. This is an anomaly in the representation; I cannot decipher the meaningfulness of the image within the context of the study of the Multimedia Super Corridor. Cricket is a popular sports in Malaysia, as well as it is in the so-called British Commonwealth in which the game has evolved into a signature sports. Baseball is definitely a popular sports in American and Japan; but not in Malaysia.

Figure 23: The Malaysian Image of Progress, Visual #4

The next image in this visual is that of the hypermodern mall that symbolizes Malaysia's Friedmanian (1982) entry into the age of mass consumption in which there is more freedom to choose out of what advertisers are offering. Indeed Friedman (1982) proposes that capitalism is about freedom and free choice. The mall is emblematic of the triumph of global corporate capitalism in that what is sold in the mall are the finished brand-named products assembled through the global production house of the sweatshops that include under-aged children employed as cheap labor. The caption of the composite image of Malaysian progress reads "To Create a City to Fulfill the Objective of Vision 2020" is a reference to the corporate Malaysia's mission statement for the creation of real estate projects in accordance to Mahathir's wishes. As discussed in the autobiographic chapter on Malaysia's prime minister, "Vision 2020" is a statement of developmentalist principles authored by the author of the MSC. In Table 4 below, I provide a summary of the semiosis of Malaysia's image of progress.

Table 5: Semiotic Analysis of the Malaysian Image of Progress

SIGN	SIGNIFIER	SIGNIFIED
Woman in a library	Learning	Knowledge society/ modernity
People in a baseball field	Playing	Foreign sports/ postmodernity
An empty shopping mall	Buying and selling	Mass or conspicuous consumption/ hypermodernity
Three Malay dancers	Entertaining/inviting	Tourism/monarchy/ Postmodernity

Visual #5, Figure 24

In Figure 24, Visual #5 below, is a semiotic reading on the theme of national development. The page contains images of hypermodernism and religious foundation. The city of Putrajaya is installed with architectural landscape that signifies Islamizing, connecting, and colonizing. The three signs — the mosque, the map of the territory and the bridge — respectively signifies the connectedness of religion, (Islam in this case,) with the new territory mapped for a new style of developmentalism. The new area is represented to be one that synthesizes the elements of creativity and ethics; of the creation of a newer form of installation and a reminder of the supremacy of Islam as Malaysia's official religion. The utopia represented is Islamic-based, although in Malaysia there are adherents to Christianity, Hinduism, Buddhism, Sikhism, Taoism, Confucianism and religions of the natives. There is another interesting linguistic or semiotic aspect to this picture; that the areas segmented for the new territory is called "precincts" There are "Civic and Cultural Precinct", "Commercial Precincts," and "Sports and Recreational Precinct". The word "precinct" is reminiscent of the one used to designate "police stations" such as those in New York City, New York, United States of America.

Exactly what the author of Malaysian Putrajaya has in mind when naming these areas is not exactly clear. The idea of "policing" however, might make sense—that this major city of the MSC is to be policed or with be controlled and surveillenced by Informational Communications Technologies; ones better than those used in the past. Whilst the informational communicational infrastructure will help in police the physical aspects of the state, religion will help "police the souls" of the people in the new city. One can apply the idea of "disciplining" (Focault, 1978) and "punishing" to the analysis of the politics and psychology of the inhabitants of the new technopole. Indeed a Focaultian reading of the city might highlight the idea of how technology and systems of control hegemonizes over human consciousness. The "panopticonism" of Putrajaya lies in the notion that the consciousness of the people is already structured to accept the idea that a hyper-modernized developmentalist project that is systemized by a synthesis of controlling tehnologies and ethics historically accepted ethics is as natural as the progression of capitalism.

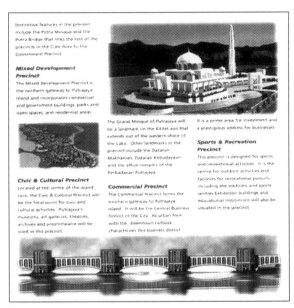

Figure 24: Spirits in a Material World, Visual #5

In Table 6, I provide a semiotic analysis of the signs, symbols, and signifier of the image of synthesis. The Malaysian utopia is presented as one that blends religious foundation and hypermodernity. In fact the philosophy pf development in Malaysia has always been the designing of systems that will put economic and religious development in balance.

Table 6: Semiotics Analysis of Spiritual-Material Installations

SIGN	SIGNIFIER	SIGNIFIED
Aerial view of coastal area	Mapping	Utopia
Mosque (*Masjid*)	Islamizing	Religious-based
Bridge	Connecting	Synthesis

Analysis of Supplementary materials

In the following paragraphs, I will discuss my reading of the images on the front cover of brochures entitled "Unlocking the potentials of the information age," (MDC, 1997) "Cyberjaya: The model intelligent city in the making" (MDC, n.d.), and "Putrajaya: The federal government administrative center" (Putrajaya Holdings, 1997). The images of the front covers are not reproduced in this study but are described below. I will first discuss the one entitled "Putrajaya: The Federal Government Administrative Capital."

Cover Page, "Putrajaya: The federal government administrative capital."

The front cover has a simple design: the word "Putrajaya" is somewhat inscribed on a light green background; a greenfield and lush tropical forest to be more specific. There is also an image of an embossed map perhaps of the new administrative capital itself. The word "Putrajaya" is an interesting hybrid of the word "Putra" (Sanskrit=prince) and "Jaya" (Sanskrit=victory). It means "victory of a prince". Presumably "Putra" is taken from one of the honorific titles of Malaysia's first prime minister, Tengku Abdul Rahman Putra AlHaj. It also means, in the Malay language, "son of a king." Related to the image of on the front cover is one that is on the inside of it; a composite image of life in the city of Putrajaya.

Cover Page "Unlocking the full potential of the information age."

The text has a dark blue background and is artistically and professionally designed. It shows the inside of a computer system, with a blow-up abstract of a binary system-with the numerals 101010 designed like a rotating metal plate. The title "Unlocking the Full Potential of Information Age" printed in bold orange (against the contrasting background of hues of dark blue) is displayed in the middle of the text. It is intended primarily for international investors. The 45-page text has a logo of the Multimedia Super Corridor at the left hand corner of the text. The phrase "Multimedia Development Corp." appears directly below the word Multimedia Super Corridor. The dark blue brochure, measuring somewhat 24 by 10 inches has a glossy feel to it. It is a finely designed brochure of which also has a corporate look and one I feel professionally produced.

On the back of the brochure is a more detailed information on its authorship. The three pieces of information is placed directly below the word Multimedia Super Corridor. The first information is that other client service department entitled application for MSC status and service inquiries for companies. It gives the address of Multimedia Development Corp. and that address is in the new business capital of Malaysia called Cyberjaya. The second information directs the reader to the corporate communications Department of the Multimedia Super Corridor and it is entitled "General and Media Inquiries." And the last piece of information is called "Other Available MSC brochures which gives information on other kinds of brochures available from the corporation.

I begin the analysis by looking at the title "Unlocking the Full Potential of The Information Age", (see Table 7) as there are of several concepts which are embedded in that particular sentence which signifiers something larger than just a clever and persuasive phrase. "Unlocking something," connotes power relations; that there is a treasure-chest of potential for those who has the key to unlock it.

Table 7: The Metaphor of "Unlocking"

"Unlocking"	Metaphor of key/ power	The MSC
The full potential	A treasure-chest of possibilities	The benefits
(of the Information Age)	A catchphrase to indicate the dawn of a new era	

The ability to unlock something entails that I can make things happen, to uncover something, and ability to be given the power to make changes so that what is desired will be attained. It also entails the opening up of new possibilities, to conjure new image of change, new dimensions of living, new existential moments, and new way of doing things. The next thing that strikes me is the word "Information Age". Taken together the word "Unlocking the Full Potential of the Information Age" signifies a futuristic dimension of being-ness, a sense of flow of entering an entirely new frame of mind, and to enter and hence exist in an Information Age whose characteristics and dimensions we are yet to define.

Looking at the brochure and also the title "Unlocking the Full Potential of Information Age" and word "Multimedia Super Corridor" itself and to try to understand the concept of "Information Age," we are actually entering not just a textual realm, but also a different perspective; semantics, semiotic, and linguistic philosophical dimension of change elaborated by the author of text. In Table 8 below I provide a summary of the reading of images from the two brochures.

Table 8: Summary of Semiotic Analysis of Two Brochures

	SIGN	SIGNIFIER	SIGNIFIED
Brochure #1 "Unlocking the Potentials of the Information Age"	Diskette/ bricolaged/ deconstructed	Cybernetics	Digital world Information Age
Brochure #2 "Intelligent City in the Making"	Super-conductivity wire/Broken/ Bricolaged /Deconstructed Broken wire over Malaysian map	High speed progress Supremacy of broadband technology over Malaysia	Hyper-development "wired world" "Digitally-driven" developmentalism

My third supplementary analysis is of the cover page of the brochure on Malaysia's Cyberjaya, from the brochure "Model intelligent city in the making,"

Cover Page, "Model intelligent city in the making."

The color of this brochure is a combination of blue and green hues of interesting complexity. Inscribed on this front cover of the brochure are very interesting signs and symbols and what they signify. The soothing and contemplative blue background has the image of an inside of a computer disk with binary numbers inscribed on it. The aerial view image of a new city in the making—lush tropical forests surrounding—can be seen down below a hovering superconductor-wire/broadband wire. This is a very interesting image of "cybernetics" as the caption reads "A Model Intelligent City in the Making". The logo of the MSC (Multimedia Development Corporation" can be seen on the right hand side below. At the bottom right hand side of the page, is the word "Cyberjaya", the name of the city.

Cyber (from Latin "Kyber") + Jaya (from Sanskrit) = Cyberjaya

The hybridity of the words signify a marriage of two cultures; Latin and Hindu-Buddhist. A study of the hybridity of the word is an important aspect of my dissertation. It embodies not only the analysis of two words, one a prefix and the other a suffix, "cyber" and "jaya" respectively, but also a study of the genealogy of two terms from two different cultural/civilizational origins that are projected in hybridity in this age characterized by the primacy of and emphasis on "digital" literacy. Cyberjaya" literally means "Cybernetics Rules" or the "Victory of Cybernetics" that creates a hypermodernized world whose creation is inspired by a digitally-driven developmentalism (Table 9).

Table 9: Characteristics of the Intelligent City

	SIGN	SIGNIFIER	SIGNIFIED
Brochure Analysis: "Model Intelligent city in the making"	Superconductivity wire/Broken/ Bricolaged /deconstructed Broken wire over Malaysian map	High speed progress Supremacy of broadband technology over Malaysia	Hyper-development "wired world" "Digitally-driven" developmentalism

In the figure presented in the front cover, there is the logo of the corporate body called "Multimedia Development Corporation," established to design and engineer the transformation. The logo of the governing body of the development of Malaysia's Multimedia Super Corridor, is science-fictionist. It looked like an approaching space ship! The name "Cyberjaya", designed in an advant garde font, also signifies an image of futurism. One might also interpret the logo as either a symbol of progress signifying the advancement of Malaysian corporate capitalism or the one may also look at it as a technologized image of an approaching "shark" of the advancing of global telematics giants, invited to advise on Malaysia's mega-technological change (international corporate developmentalist sharks approaching?)

In Table 10 below, I present the relationship between what is termed as an "intelligent city," and its properties, as conceived in the case of Cyberjaya. The idea of an "intelligent city" signifies a new genre of cities that surpass "less intelligent" ones. Intelligence here is equated with the use of "digital communication" technologies to gain access to the services provided. One may for example, use "smart cards" to gain access to "smart buildings" or to "smart homes" and send children to "smart schools." The table below (Table 10) illustrates the relationship between the word intelligent city and the subdivisions it produces.

Table 10: Semiotics of Intelligent City in the Making

"Intelligent City" (Cyberjaya)	Run on fiber optics
	Have "intelligent buildings"
	Uses "smart cards"
	"computational technology" driven

The word "model" in the phrase "model intelligent city in the making" is a reference to many other cities like Cyberjaya planned for the entire state of Malaysia. Malaysia has thirteen state capitals altogether and if all of these are to undergo an ideological and infrastructural migration as such, there will be the need to create twenty six intelligent cities (one administrative and one economic capital). From the representation of the concept of social change, derived from the two brochures we can find the theme of technological fantasy of a world of peace, plenty, and prosperity, based on the supremacy of "cybernetics" as infrastructural enabler.

Intertextuality

The range of intertexts embedded in the main brochure analyzed, as well as in the front-cover presentation of the three supporting brochures are broad.

By intertextuality (Kristeva, 1984) I mean the idea of how one idea is semantically linked to another. As in the case of the brochures and the themes form the speeches on Cyberjaya,", here are my main observations as the relate to Mahathir's vision, the creation of the new Malaysia, and the brochures concerning social change:

1. In the brochure "Malaysia in the new Millennium," the two pages of visuals selected comprise of images of development and progress is advertised. The inspiration for the authorship of course comes from the paradigm of development embraced by the Malaysian government under the rule of Mahathir Mohamad. The images point out to the idea of a program of economic, social, and cultural development that synthesizes homegrown as well as foreign-imported ideas. The text (the composite images) and the sub-texts (details in the compositions) point to the idea of intertextuality in that the Malaysian image of progress looks like a replication of the image of the advancement in the Western capitalist nations. The images represent a showcase of corporate capitalist development that is also pegged to modern interpretation of Islam. In the language of intertextuality, the images also represent or signify the nation's reliance on ideas and implementation of progress from the West. The image of the infrastructures in the Malaysian Multimedia Super Corridor Project portray a synthesis of borrowed ideas that are semantically link or inter-textualized to another.

2. in the brochure "Unlocking the Potentials of the Information age", the production of signs and

symbols is related to the image of a computerized world. Computer technology originated from the Pentagon or the Department of Defense of the United States of America; a technology originally developed for the purpose of advancing military technology or specifically to have computers "talk to each other" so that they can better navigate missiles. The image of a world that is dark blue in nature is linked to the idea of a "unified" world in harmony with the forces of the "digital" world. The world is interpreted as closely linked to unity, peace, and plenty once the potentials of the Information Age is unlocked.

3. in the brochure "The model intelligent city in the making, "the signs and symbols produced is even more complex. The sign of the superconductivity wire relates to the world of networking and "wiring up" which has its origin in the Silicon Valley, California" generally and of the major corporation Cisco Systems in particular, the latter a company which has global dominance in its business of installing fiber-optic networks. The image of a pleasing green background that has Malaysia hovered over by the broken wire, is an intertextual moment of the colonizing properties of technology over a sovereign state.

4. in the last brochure "Putrajaya: the new state administrative capital", word "Putrajaya" which signifies a new city taken from the name of a Malay prince who became Malaysia's first Prime Minister can be linked intertextually to the idea of a new wave of "Independence". Malaysia gained independence from the British in 1957 and in

1997 (the year the Multimedia Super Corridor is conjured), forty years after that a "newer" independence is conjured. Hence, the text "Putrajaya" signifies a new wave of independence; akin to an ideological migration.

Summary: Semantic Representation of Themes from Inscription #1

In the brief notes, below I summarize the findings on my semiotic reading select images of the brochures:

1. To "unlock potentials" mean to discover the magic of Informational and Communication technologies and the design national developmental policies that would enable the adoption of the ideology of "digitally-driven" developmentalism that would consequently aid the country in its path to "hypermodernity";

2. To "discover the magic: means to develop the nation technologically by the installing The Multimedia Super Corridor and to discover the magic of the marketplace of global capitalism that puts emphasis on computer-related technologies as products of world consumption;

3. To" install a new ideology" means to migrate. This means to move the administrative and economic capitals of Kuala Lumpur to two industrial complexes, Putrajaya (administrative) and Cyberjaya (economic), so that the country can better meet the needs of the global capitalists that is believed to be able to help in Malaysia's national development;

4. To progress means to maintain cultural roots and present a hypermodern image of culture that is attractive to tourists and hence to tourism; that culture in the new agenda of developmentalism will be further relegated to "showcase culture" and becomes an industry in itself;

5. To progress means to adopt values that are brought in *via* foreign investment albeit subconsciously, enabled by the dissemination of expressions of ideology that emanates from the cultural industrial complexes such as American, European, or Japanese economic and cultural institutions.

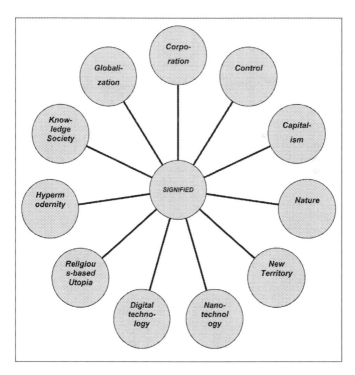

Figure 25: Signifieds

Conclusion: Significations and their Significance

From the findings of this study of inscriptions (in the form of corporate brochures) I conclude that the images presented in these publications represent that of a hyper-modernized nation desperate to ride the wave of globalization by engineering a synthesis of nationalism and hypermodernity. The driving force is informational communication technology believed to be able to help Malaysia become noticed by the advanced capitalist nations. The attention is needed to attract foreign investment so that the national development agenda can continue to be carried out.

As represented in the table below (Table 10) in the catalog of themes I gathered from the study of "signs, signified and signifiers," the image of progress is a kaleidoscope of themes that have the dimensions of "conditions" and "consequences." By "conditions," I mean the "conditions" needed for Malaysia's development, such as the need to adopt the ideology of corporate capitalism, to computerize, and to move into a new era of possibilities driven by digital communication technologies. By "consequences" I mean the urge for the government to engineer change from modernity to postmodernity with Islam as the guiding religion by virtue of its status as an official religion. The consequences of development will thus be a utopia of the Information Age, governed by Constitutional Monarchy and in harmony with nature but yet linked to global economic forces and one that will also promote the culture of mass consumption.

Table 11: Summary of Themes from the Information
in the Brochures

Computerization	Modernity	New era
Control	Postmodernity	Information Age
Corporate Capitalism	Knowledge Society	Possibilities
Corporation	Monarchy	"Wired" world
Finance	Foreign Sports	Mass Consumption
Globalization	Nano-technology	Synthesis
Nature	Transit	Religious-based
New Territory	Utopia	Digitally-driven
One-dimensionalization	Tourism	Hyper-development

In the next chapter on the next set of inscriptions, I will discuss the themes of Prime Ministerial speeches that concern Malaysia's MSC project.

Chapter VIII

Inscription #2: Analysis of speech texts

Introduction

In this chapter, I discuss Prime Ministerial speeches as they relate to the development of Cyberjaya and the Multimedia Super Corridor. I highlight the major themes that emerge out of my analysis of the speeches. The most common themes mentioned in the speeches are "Technological Determinism and/or Technological Progress" (Table 17) that appears throughout the 21 speeches. The tables below elaborate the sub themes of each of the findings. I provide exemplifying quotes from the speeches. I discuss the select sub themes and weave them in each section (see Appendix C for complete set of themes and subthemes) I conclude this chapter with a discussion of what these findings mean and how they relate to one another.

Counter-hegemony

In Table 12 below, the evidence that shows Malaysia's awareness of the hegemony of the advanced industrialized nations lie in the country's awareness of its counter-hegemonic strategies. In my analysis, counter-hegemony as a theme is supported by the saturatedness of the sub-themes such as the need to be a "global producer" of multimedia products, to be competitive globally, to create a sense of "regional nationalism," and to strive for "universal access to technology." The MSC is also created as Malaysia's strategy "to reap the benefits" of the Information Age. There is the awareness of the "ethics of technological determinism" in that technology is not necessarily a life force in itself and can be used in an equitable way. Hence, the theme of awareness, which I interpret as counter-hegemony, is supported by select subthemes/codes derived from speeches.

Table 12: On Awareness/Counter-hegemony

AWARENESS OF/ COUNTER-HEGEMONY	1] Malaysia just celebrated its 42 years of independence last month. Within that time span the world saw Malaysia transformed from an agro-based economy to an industrial-based entity, swiftly moving into high-tech and plunging into the information age. p. 9: UcapanCyberjaya8.txt—9:1 (16:20)
	2] The United States has been around for over 200 years, and within that period, its society has gone through a process of social, cultural, economic and political change which had transformed it from a newly independent backward country into the richest and the most powerful nation that it is today. p. 9: UcapanCyberjaya8.txt—9:8 (55:60)

In Table 13 below, I further emphasize the theme of counter-hegemony. To counter hegemonize, the MSC is build to first create knowledge workers who will help Malaysia become a regional leader and a global participant in the Information Age. Through education and with the use of Informational Communication Technologies, the country is hoping to create a competitive edge in the contemporary world economy.

Table 13: On Counter-hegemony

COUNTER HEGEMONY	1] Dalam hal ini, kita tidak mempunyai pilihan melainkan kita sanggup ditinggal di belakang, menjadi miskin dan akibatnya terpaksa tunduk kepada kehendak orang lain. 1] In this sense, we do not have any choice, unless we chose to be left behind and impoverished and as a consequence, subjugated to the needs of others. p. 3: cyberjaya2.txt—3:50 (69:72) 2] Daya saing ekonomi negara di masa depan bergantung kepada kesediaan kita untuk menggunakan IT dan menjadi pekerja berilmu. 2] In future, the nation's competitive edge will be dependent upon our willingness to use Informational Technology and to become "knowledgeable workers." p. 3: cyberjaya2.txt—3:18 (78:80)

Globalization

In table 14 below, the theme "globalization" produce subthemes that illustrate Malaysia's perception of what the phenomena of globalization is. There is a paradox in the conceptualization in that "globalization" connotes the idea of "collaboration" but driven by the philosophy of technological determinism; "multicultural synthesis" yet driven by "global competition, "participation" yet relegating the nation to the status of a technological "test bed" for multinational corporations.

Table 14: On Globalization

GLOBALIZATION	1] Cyberjaya will be a unique blend of the best from East and West evolving to take on its own creative culture. p. 2: UcapanCyberjaya1.txt—2:29 (207:208)

Hegemony

In Table 15 below, the dominant theme of "hegemony" produces subthemes such as "advisory panel," "technological consciousness,""Center-Periphery," and "Developmentalism." The level of hegemony that characterizes the MSC project and how it operates is varied; they operate from the level of "developmentalist" ideology, to the "Center-Periphery" economic relationship; "technological consciousness" generated; and the International Advisory Panel producing the ideologies. These are complex levels of hegemony I discern from the themes of the speeches. They permeate throughout the thinking of those in power who create the project.

Table 15: On Hegemony

HEGEMONY	1] The Multimedia Super Corridor which we created is acknowledged by people in the industry as unique. The International Advisory Panel on which sit most of the successful people involved in multimedia business, research and development has enabled us to keep track of the latest thinking and advances in the Information Age and to make provision for them in terms of cyber laws, practices, infrastructure needs and policies. p. 9: UcapanCyberjaya8.txt—9:16 (168:175) 2] In Malaysia, we are creating the Multimedia Super Corridor to harness these new forces. We hope this will accelerate our economic development and create exciting opportunities that our international partners cannot pursue elsewhere. p. 6: UcapanCyberjaya5.txt—6:11 (51:55)

National Strategy

In Table 16 below, I present the subthemes that relates to the main theme of "national" in the collection of speeches on Cyberjaya and MSC analyzed. The idea economic nationalism is translated to mean having the confidence to as a sovereign nation that takes pride in being a producer of the world market, that the pride comes from the government's success in producing good workers in the computer technology sector, and that the MSC is created as a national strategy for high speed economic growth. The MSC is a national priority project since it will create a better sense of nationalism through resource mobilization as a national agenda.

Table 16: On National (Strategy)

NATIONAL	1] Our comprehensive and integrated strategy has attracted various world statesmen and business leaders who have personally visited Cyberjaya to witness the MSC experiment. The MSC, as a catalyst for growth and global test-bedding, has also spawned numerous similar initiatives around the globe. p. 2: UcapanCyberjaya1.txt—2:14 (90:96) 2] Pentingnya IT sebagai teknologi strategik tidak boleh dinafikan. IT bukan sahaja kunci kepada meningkat daya saing Malaysia di pasaran dunia, tetapi juga cara utama bagi mencapai matlamat-matlamat Wawasan 2020. 2] The importance of Informational Technology as strategic technology cannot be denied. It is not only the key to Malaysia's competitiveness in the world market but also as a means to achieve the objectives of Vision 2020. p. 3: cyberjaya2.txt—3:52 (157:161)

Technological Determinism

In Table 17 below, I present the two most saturated themes: technological determinism and technological progress. "Technological determinism" especially drives the developmentalist agenda and determines the nature of hegemony and utopianism of this Southeast Asian state. The saturatedness of the theme offer the conclusion to this study that there is strong sense in the regime of Mahathir that the reliance on informational and communication technologies (ICT) is almost of total dependence politically and the belief in technology possessing a life-force in itself is almost religious.

Hence, national development policies is based and superstructured on technological determinism.

Table 17: On Technological Determinism/Progress
(Most saturated themes)

TECHNOLOGICAL DETERMINISM

1] The information age demands that second wave technologies be transformed into new industrial structures associated with what are today called "webs".
 p. 1: infotech malaysia 96.txt - 1:8 (53:56)

2] It was only a few years ago that we were so engrossed with the manufacturing industry and, hardly have fully extended it when we find ourselves in the information age.
 p. 9: UcapanCyberjaya8.txt - 9:3 (22:25)

3] Before our very eyes, the typewriter has become obsolete, the fax machine will eventually face the same fate and e-mail, which used to be an astonishing
fascination only just six years ago, has now become as common as posting a letter.
 p. 9: UcapanCyberjaya8.txt - 9:4 (27:31)

Utopianism

Finally, in Table 18 below, I present an elaborate list of subthemes of the nature of utopia that is created out of the MSC. The government perceives the Malaysian utopian as one that can be part of the "electronic village," is "eco-friendly," and governed by digital communication technologies. Informational and communication technologies are to be used as a technology to enable the creation of a "civil society," that will also help create an investment haven for multinational corporation—true to the ideology of corporate capitalism. The MSC is a utopia of "knowledge workers" who live in an "information-rich" knowledge society in a nation that is "networked" to other civilizational centers of the region and the world. The new world is to be ruled by the wise and one that will see the development of participatory democracy that uses computer technology as an ideological state apparatus. This Stanford University—inspired, Silicon Valley—modeled utopia is one that promotes the idea of world peace through collaborations in the world economy in which everybody wins (win-win world economy)

Table 18: On Utopia

UTOPIA	1] Masyarakat ini juga akan menjadi lebih matang, liberal, demokratik, toleran, prihatin dan adil kedudukan ekonominya—satu masyarakat yang diimpikan oleh Wawasan 2020. 1] This society will also become more mature, liberal, democratic, tolerant, emphatic, and just in its economic standing—a society dreamed of by Vision 2020. p. 3: cyberjaya2.txt—3:37 (196:199) 2] With the MSC we are actually creating an investment haven in the middle of palm oil plantations to usher in the third wave of information and knowledge industries. p. 1: infotech malaysia 96.txt—1:23 (216:219) 3] We must be able to produce individuals who are able to leverage on intellectual capital in order to move from concept to explicit knowledge and thereafter, the production of next generation products and services. p. 7: UcapanCyberjaya6.txt—7:45 (204:208) 4] A civil society of the future must be a society where the wise rule and the people actively participate in determining their destiny. p. 1: infotech malaysia 96.txt—1:17 (141:143)

Themes from Findings

I analyzed 21 speeches concerning Cyberjaya and the MSC, drawing out initial themes and spelling out codes that are then analyzed for their saturatedness and their groundedness. The important and recurring ones were then drawn out so that they would be interlinked. The following are the major themes derived from the coding processes (initial and axial) from the 21 Prime Ministerial speeches on the Multimedia Super Corridor. The following major themes (summarized in Table 19) emerge:

Table 19: Themes from the speeches of Mahathir Mohamad

Economics	Globalization	Hegemony	Knowledge Society	National	Paradigm
Revolution	Ruling Government	Utopia	Worldview	Ideology	Digital Proletarianism
Technological determinism	Awareness or 'Counter Hegemony'	Civil Society	Counter-hegemony	Cyber-related themes	

If we frame these general themes within the cyclical mode of technology, ideology, politics, and hegemony, we will discern the idea that technological determinism drives the ideology of developmentalism and determine the politics of cultural reconfiguration and hence characterize the nature of hegemony. A further elaboration of the point above would catalog the following themes as in Table 20 below:

Table 20: More specific themes from the speeches

Scientific rationalism	Migration
Scientism	Nationalism
Historical-materialism	Divide and rule
National identity	Anti-Westernism
Control	Digital proletarianism
Authoritarianism	

In Figure 26 below I suggest how hegemonizing forces operate. From the findings on the themes drawn from the speeches, I conclude that the root of hegemonic formulations lies in the philosophy of cyberneticism that transmutates and transmigrate from the level of philosophy to the level of the creation of a state based on cybernetic principles. This conclusion is consistent with the saturatedness of the theme "technological determinism" or "technological progress" that define the developmentalist agenda of Malaysia. In the next chapter to further enrich the explanation on the transcultural flow of hegemony, I will discuss how ideology becomes installations and how it defines the new landscape of the country and subsequently alters the social relations of production based on the demands of the new "scriptural economy" (de Certeau, 1984)

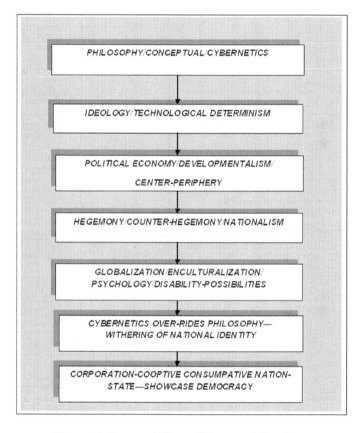

Figure 26: Structural Flow of Hegemonizing Forces

Chapter IX

Inscription #3: Analysis of Landscape

Introduction

In this chapter, I look at how the idea of "cybernetics" trickle down" to the masses. I will discuss how popular images of the so-called "Cybernetic Age" gets inscribed onto the landscape. The idea of technological fantasy and "linguistic hybridity" particularly will be illustrated here as a further illustration of the concept of hegemony and technological determinism.

Images of production and reproduction/ Cyberneticism Trickles Down

I assembled a composite select images of the character of Malaysia's transformation; a collage of, in the broadest sense of the word, social production and reproduction through education. Beginning our analysis of signs and symbols of the picture on the left and on to the last one on the bottom right, I see a continuity of images that can be related in a complex manner. The banner reads "Persidangan dan Expo Internet Tamil Terbesar di Dunia." Translated as "The World's Biggest Tamil Internet Conference and Exposition". Tamil is a vernacular language spoken by a majority of Malaysian Indians that are, up to the writing of this dissertation, politically represented by the Malaysian Indian Congress.

On the right-hand side of the picture we see an aerial view of the higher institution Malaysian Multimedia University, a private institution that focuses on granting undergraduate and graduate degrees in "multimedia sciences." The name Multimedia University is unique in the sense that it does not immortalize or memorialize persons or place or event in history but rather a "product," an "artifact," or "an approach of looking at things." "Multimedia", consistent with the need to align with a center of production called the Multimedia Super Corridor, means more than one medium and the emphasis here is to highlight a university specialization that produces "multimedia products." The product or artifact includes CD-ROMS, Websites, or any other products that integrates text, hypertext, audio, and video. Graduates of The Multimedia University pride themselves as the first to be awarded diplomas in the form of "digital diplomas." The Chancellor of the university is the Prime Minister's wife, Siti Hasmah Ali.

The picture on the middle left is that of the (formerly) tallest building in the world: The Petronas Twin Tower. "Petronas" means "Petroliam Nasional" or "National Petrolium" which means the national oil company. It is a said to be a symbol of Malaysian nationalism and economic power. On the right I present a picture of people looking at the twin towers. The towers seem to be a spectacle of a spectre that haunts the world of informational capitalism, and that attract spectators. I took this picture when I was doing my observation at the foot of the twin towers.

I do not know the significance of "twin towers" but there seems to be an obsession to imitate the style of architecture of the Western world; particularly of postmodernism as pioneered perhaps by those working in the International Style (Le Corboursier). The naming of names in Malaysia is plagued with the desire to compete with world's establishes signs and symbols and the desire to project the image of economic success through architectural feats. The Petronas Twin Towers is in fact used as a scene of a movie called *The Entrapment* (Connery, Hertzberg, & Tollefson, producers, 2000); one about conspiracy and robbery of a sophisticated nature, involving international robber barons. This is a form of Hollywood-styled advertising for a nation such as Malaysia that wishes to attract foreign investment.

The picture in Figure 21, shows respectively images of children coming back/going home from school and an Internet café, or what is also known as "cybercafe." Both are images of production and reproduction. One goes to school to learn about the world, the disciplines or the subject matter including "Computer Science" or in Malay "Sains Komputer" and one goes to Internet cafes to hone the skills of "surfing the Net" and "playing online games" as what the cafes are famous for. The cafes are also extremely popular with users who love to "chat." If in France during the Renaissance period cafes intellectuals gather in cafes and salons to exchange revolutionary ideas, in Malaysian cafes, they are popular with people chatting without speaking.

Figure 27: Images of Production and Reproduction

Images of Digital Proletarianism

Figure 28 below shows an inscription in the form of a typical modern–day Malaysian school building. During my fieldwork in August, I stayed at my sister's house in front of this school. This is a typical look of a new school building in Malaysia. The discourse on "Smart Schools", or schools that uses technology-rich environment of learning, pervades the educational system, reminiscence of the development of American education in the 1980s with the emphasis on the production of computer literate workers (see Gross & Gross, Eds., 1985.) The inscription on the wall says "(Bangunan) Multimedia Utama" or "Main Multimedia (Building)." The secondary (or high) school is a natural passage for social reproduction for Malaysia's "quantum leap" into the Information Age. Across the street is a highway and a popular strip for 'drag racers' consisting of youths who perhaps worked menial jobs/contract laborers. In this case I saw predominantly Malaysian of Indian origin (Malaysian Indians).

Figure 28: Schooling as a cybernetic reproduction

Themes from Findings

In the images above, I discover the idea of how cybernetics is systematically trickled down. In the section of literature review, I discuss the genealogy of the concept of cybernetics as an idea of feedback loop and the innerworkings of living systems. In the case of Malaysia's transformation, the idea that cybernetic technology primarily the Internet will bring progress and liberation through the process of education is promoted by the government through policies and practice. In the following and last chapter on inscriptions, I illustrate the changing landscape of Malaysia as a consequence of the adoption of the capitalist mode of development. The nature of capitalism is one to the complexity of the world economy; a globalized world of the movement of people, trade, goods, services, and ideas that has characterized the world economy since perhaps, the collapse of the Soviet Empire.

Chapter X

Inscription #4, Stanford-ization and McDonaldizatiON of malaysia: On the political-economy of large scale inscriptions

The presence of MMU, Tenaga University and Universiti Putra Malaysia will seek to emulate the Stanford—inspired setting of Silicon Valley and create a networked, creative and productive society in Cyberjaya.

—Mahathir Mohamad

Introduction

In this fourth analytical and last section on inscriptions, I will discuss the concept of political economy and how the idea of Silicon Valley gets enculturalized and become a model for the development of Malaysia's Multimedia Super Corridor. "Large scale" inscriptions means real estate projects; physical spaces constructed out of the need for institutions to continue to express ideologies. I will present illustrations from photos of landscape and from policy speeches on how the Multimedia Super Corridor is modeled after the area popularly known as "Silicon Valley" in California. Because these illustrations are derived from policy speeches of the Prime Minister, they is a strong evidence of the roots of what I call the "Stanford-ization" (after the name Stanford University) of Malaya. Images of how "foreign signs and symbols" get inscribed onto Malaysia will be presented. I will also discuss the phenomena of the installation of primarily American "consumer-cultural symbols" onto the landscape—symbols that are part of the global capitalist "cultural-industrial" complex that become also, part of the mental inscriptions of hypermodernizing societies such as Malaysia.

Data from Speeches

I extracted 13 quotations and present below six of the most salient ones from the initial theme "Utopia: Stanford-inspired" and drew the conclusion that what is inscribed is a system of practices that is modeled after the success of the American cybernetics industry, whose seeds of growth were planted by research enterprise at Stanford University, Palo Alto, California. The references of the quotes are written in the form as they appear from the archive of the Grounded Theory software I use.

Theme: Stanford–Inspired Utopia

The themes from the quotes in Table 21 suggest strongly that Malaysia's Multimedia Super Corridor is indeed a replica of the economic/cultural—industrial complex that exist in California.

Table 21: Stanford-Inspired Utopia

UTOPIA: STANFORD-INSPIRED	The presence of MMU, Tenaga University and Universiti Putra Malaysia will seek to emulate the Stanford—inspired setting of Silicon Valley and create a networked, creative and productive society in Cyberjaya. p. 2: UcapanCyberjaya1.txt—2:25 (198:202)
	It is designed to spawn creative ideas and technopreneurs—very much like the role that Stanford University plays in the success of the Silicon Valley. p. 7: UcapanCyberjaya6.txt—7:10 (32:35)
	This week, we have enjoyed an overwhelmingly positive response from the entertainment companies in Southern California and the high technology companies we saw at Stanford. p. 8: UcapanCyberjaya7.txt—8:3 (12:15)
	The MSC is not just a physical location, or just another industrial or technology park—and it is not a Far Eastern imitation of the Silicon Valley—it represents a new paradigm in the creation of value for the Information Age. p. 13: UcapanCyberjaya12.txt—13:14 (81:85)

	The concept has been based on the experience of Silicon Valley and Route 128, the growth of ICT and the dynamism generated from the convergence of computing, telecommunications and content. We have not replicated the growth models of these hubs but we have innovated and advanced further on the basis of our interaction with the industries and the MSC's International Advisory Panel members. p. 22: UcapanCyberjaya20.txt—22:3 (17:25)
	The necessary core elements are the encouragement of corporate R&D; the setting up of a new Multimedia University (MMU); and the development of large-scale R&D pilot projects. p. 22: UcapanCyberjaya20.txt—22:22 (116:120)

Theme: National Strategy/Test-bed

The quotations I extract below suggest how much Malaysia is valued as a sovereign nation; in that the creation of the MSC and the agenda to transform the economy is announced to the international investors as an opportunity for the international venture capitalists to exploit the labor, operate at the most minimal cost, and to test their products before they are produced en masse (and re-sold to the Third Word countries).

Table 22: National Test-bed

NATIONAL STRATEGY: TESTBED	These companies are also looking for a platform to test their products and ideas. p. 1: infotech malaysia 96.txt—1:48 (244:246)

	Now we are aiming to be a major player in Information
	Age industry. For this we will welcome with open arms foreign investments. Those who have experience doing business in Malaysia know that we are ever willing to listen and to act to meet the multifarious needs of foreign investors. And so the Multimedia Super Corridor is created to become a giant test-bed for the soft and hard products of the cyber age.
	  p. 9: UcapanCyberjaya8.txt—9:20
	                    (226:234) (emphasis added)

	What the companies learn and test in the MSC will help prepare them to solve problems faced when applying their technologies and expertise worldwide. p. 16: UcapanCyberjaya15.txt—16:20 (95:97)
	Since we are literally moving into the unknown and we expect rapid and radical changes it is prudent to test our ideas first before implementing them nation-wide to avoid costly mistakes. Hence, the MSC as a test-bed. p. 20: UcapanCyberjaya18.txt—20:28 (91:95

Hence the themes "Stanford–inspired utopia," and "national test-bed," drawn from speeches on the MSC illustrate the desperation by the Malaysian government, not only to bring in foreign investment and to have international venture capitalists to operate most profitably, but also to relegate the sovereign nation to the status of a "national test-bed". The model of the growth of informational capitalism of the Silicon Valley growth area; a high technology economic area whose growth was aided by the research institution, Stanford University. In Malaysia, the role of the Multimedia University mimics that of Stanford. I present below a discussion on this specialized (multimedia) university.

Figure 29 below shows the main entrance of Malaysia's new university called "Multimedia University" or Universiti Multimedia. Ideological state apparatus in the form of a highly specialized university which has become an icon of "cybernetic philosophy of education" drawing other subdivisions in education (primary, secondary, vocational) into the technicist and utilitarianistic paradigm of human development. Multimedia University is an upgraded version of Malaysia's Telecommunications Training College, which operated from Bukit Bruang, Melaka. Melaka is a historic city—the earliest Malay kingdom was called Melaka, established circa 1400. There is then a theme of migration, from Melaka to Cyberjaya, i.e. a quantum leap from ancient to post-modern. In the United States, Stanford University existed before the creation of Silicon Valley. Technological development is a process of a natural outgrowth or the enculturalization of technology facilitated by entrepreneurship. In Malaysia, the Multimedia University was created/installed to spur the growth of Malaysia's Multimedia Super Corridor. There is then an inversion of the concept of development vis-à-vis research universities in the United States that helped spur the growth of technopoles.

In the proceeding paragraphs on the "signs and symbols" in the campus of the Multimedia University, I present a more detailed discussion on the mechanism of hegemonic formation by way of the marriage of words derived from Western idea of "cybernetics" with those derived from the host/recipient culture of the Malays.

Figure 29: Entrance Of Malaysia's Multimedia University

Signs and Symbols at the Malaysian Multimedia University Campus

Inscribed onto the concrete block are names of streets buildings in the campus of Multimedia University. The first two pictures show a hybrid of Malays and Latin words. They are "Lorong Germanium" and "Persiaran Neuron" which respectively means "Germanium Avenue" and "Neuron Walk/Street". In the next two pictures in the middle of the page is an inscription of the names of facilities that are available; from living quarters to sports fields. From top to bottom, we can see a hybrid of words namely, "Pangsapuri Zeta, Eta, Upsilon, and Iota" meaning Zeta, Eta, Upsilon, and Iota Apartments, Bangunan Theta meaning "Theta

Building", Kolej Sigma and Omega meaning Sigma and Omega Colleges (Faculties), Kompleks Sukan Omicron meaning Omicron Sports Complex, and The MSC Incubator. In the last two pictures the inscriptions on the huge concrete block reads "Bangunan Beta" or "Beta Building", "Perpustakaan Delta" or "Delta Library" and finally "Cybercafe Tau" or "Tau Cybercafe".

The last picture is a religious installation on the campus of the university: a "masjid" or a mosque. The composite picture of the inscriptions and installations reveal the nature of ideological formulation that is operating at the level of education as social and cultural reproduction. The institution called The Malaysian Multimedia University was created as a response to the needs of the ideology of technological determinism and as a reproductive environment to create individuals who will continue to institutionalize capitalism and to continue onwards to the march of cybernetics capitalism. But there is also the idea of Islam as an institution that mediates the excess of capitalist developmentalism. My reading of these images inform me that the institutions were created first to disseminate the ideology of cybernetic capitalism under the shibboleth of corporate capitalism that is hegemonizing the world systems.

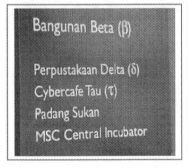

Figure 30: Inscriptions and Installations on the MMU Campus

Data from Select Photos: From Stanfordization to McDonaldization

In the above section, I discuss the hybridity of language in that are inscribed onto the landscape of the Malaysian Multimedia University. Synthesis of words are formed and inscribed onto the signs and symbols that show the direction of facilities in the building. These hybrids signify the localization of the idea that is dominant: technological determinism. They honor and celebrate the philosophy of cybernetics as a driving force of the developmentalist philosophy of this nation under transformation.

In the composite picture below (Figure 31), I gather another set of signs and symbols that are installed in the city of the old capital of Kuala Lumpur, in an area that is popular with tourists: The Bintang Walk at Jalan Bukit Bintang. The signs and symbols are, from left to right and top to bottom are that of McDonalds, Tower Records, Hard Rock Cafe, Planet Hollywood, Starbucks, and Marriott Hotel. They are distinctively American in symbolism and dominance. These are the icons of American capitalism. I call these American cultural-industrial complexes to give the idea that from these institutions, the values of consumerism are permeated to the consciousness of the people of the host and that the nations and through the process too the notion of "American democracy" is projected as an image of "freedom and the ethos of the free world of the West". I call them "cultural-industrial complexes" because through these institutions, they give expression to the nature of consumerist values that are to be sold to the host nations The values then create the culture of consumerism and in the long run, culture in the form of food, music, leisure, tourism, and ways of "doing things in one's culture" becomes an industry. Hence, from institutions to expressions, to the production of values, the nation gets to feel what an American consumerist culture is like. The feeling becomes manufactured as an industry and in the long run, when culture of this nature hegemonizes, it becomes part of the one-dimensionalization of society that will help facilitate the erosion of traditional values that have its roots in local traditions primarily expressed generation after generation through language.

Figure 31: American Cultural-Industrial Complexes

The symbol of nationalism

The twin towers of Petronas or the Petronas Twin Towers (Figure 32 below) represents a cultural and national symbol par excellence as compared to the symbols of Standfordization and McDonaldization of Malaysia. It was designed by Cesar Pelli, an American architect (Pelli,

2003) of Argentinian origin. The towers of Petronas were built by Japanese and South Korean engineers respectively; in what was a competition to see who would finish first. The inspiration to name them twin towers probably came from the idea of the twin towers of The World Trade Center in New York City destroyed on September 11, 2001. The nationalism of the creation of the towers is an inter-textualized one; the influences are global in nature.

Figure 32: The Petronas Twin Towers

Themes from Inscription #4: Standfordization of Malaysia

Figure 33 below summarizes the themes I discern from my reading of signs and symbols in the process of Standfordization and McDonaldization of Malaysia. The Center-Periphery Matrix represents the nature of hybridity and inter-textuality of the phenomena of change in this developing nation.

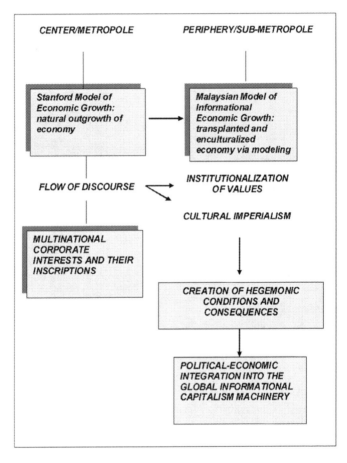

Figure 33: Centre-Periphery Matrix of the MSC

PART 4

DISCUSSION

Chapter XI

Conclusion: On Hegemony and Utopianism

" . . . the move from Kuala Lumpur to Putrajaya is more than a physical migration. It is also symbolic of discarding old legacies and old mindsets—a move towards information—driven frameworks for performance-based management and services."

— Prime Minister of Malaysia

Introduction

In the introductory chapter, I stated my intention to explore the nature of hegemony and utopianism. In this chapter on the major findings of this study, we will look at the ensemble of themes that has emerged from the preceding analyses; themes such as technological determinism, awareness, hegemony, cybernetics, national strategy, developmentalist paradigm, and utopianism. How might technological determinism as a dominant theme is counter-balanced with the question of "awareness" and "counter-hegemony" so that a certain kind of Southeast Asian—styled utopianism is manifested in the grand Malaysian real estate project? The figure below illustrate an initial finding before we proceed to the level of deep structuring of hegemony and counter-hegemony. Below is a summary of findings from the analytical chapters on "Inscriptions":

From the chapter on Mahathir as text, I discover the dimension of "authoritarianism" in the analysis of how one man's ideas get inscribed onto the consciousness of the people governed. Approaching the analysis of authoritarianism from the point of view of The Evolving Systems Approach, I looked at the genealogy of authoritarianism. The author's personal history plays a very important role in his development as an authoritarian leader. The success of the installation of the Malaysian Multimedia Super Corridor can be attributed largely to the nature of the authoritarian rule that has characterized the political culture of Malays specifically and Malaysians in general.

From the chapter on Inscription #1, I discover the themes of hypermodernity in Malaysia's development projects. Using semiotic analysis, I discover that the images represented and significant to the analysis point explained the idea of progress as a political, social, cultural, and economic migration. The technological fantasy embedded in the images are characteristic of the fantasy of a nation wanting to be like the nation of hypermodern colonists such as the United States and Japan and believing that informational communication technologies will be bring peace, plenty, and prosperity to the nation.

From the chapter on Inscription #2, I discover the importance of the ideology of "technological progress and technological determinism" as a twin concept that fuel the engine of Malaysia's economic growth. Technological determinism is the belief that technology is a life force in itself and national development policies must be authored based on this belief system. Through the detailed analyses of prime ministerial speech texts, I discerned other major themes such as hegemony and counter-hegemony, as well as globalization and nationalism that define the character of the study.

From the chapter on Inscription #3, I discover how ideas get inscribed onto the physical landscape and then becomes institutions of control that will then continue to hegemonize in newer forms. Through the analysis of picture I took of strategic areas in The MSC, I discover the pervasiveness of the signs and symbols of Western capitalist interests that continue to colonize the spaces. I discover the role of language as a powerful restructuring tool in the case of Malaysia's Multimedia University. The street names reflect the interest in hegemonizing the philosophy of cyberneticism and to further celebrate the march of informational capitalism.

From the chapter on Inscription #4, I discover the idea of cultural and industrial complexes that have become installations in the area of the Super Corridor. American business interests populate the area. The idea of Stanford University as an inspiration for the MSC point to the idea of Stanfordization of Malaysia; that the base and superstructure of the nation is, albeit claims to economic nationalism, fundamentally an appropriation of Western corporate capitalism.

Figure 34 below summarizes the hegemonic relationship in that from the philosophy of cybernetics, the influence of technological determinism as ideology, and the tensions created in the global economy, hegemony is maintained by the advanced nations over developing nation such as Malaysia. In response to the hegemony that is prevailing, a nation such as Malaysia creates a utopia called The Multimedia Super

Corridor based on the philosophy of cybernetics, taking into consideration the challenges of the global economy. The counter-hegemonic act creates a blend of utopian nationalism, at least at the time of its creation. It is not however clear what the outcome of the battle between the nation and the unseen forces of globalization that runs on a high-speed version of capitalism.

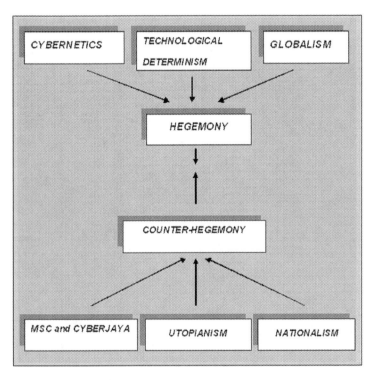

Figure 34: Co relationships of Hegemony

Theme: Technological Determinism

In Table 23 below I highlight some of the salient instances from the collection of speeches that show the idea of technological determinism as a driving force in the case of the creation of the Malaysian Multimedia Super Corridor.

Table 23: Technological Determinism

Technological Determinism	With the convergence of computing, telecommunications and broadcasting in the multimedia industry, it is now imperative that we develop our own socio-technical capability for a smoother transition into the information age. p. 1: infotech malaysia 96.txt—1:6 (39:43)
	Revolusi ini sedang mempercepatkan lagi proses globalisasi, mencorak semula ekonomi kita dan mempengaruhi cara hidup kita dan cara kita bekerja. *This revolution is speeding up the process of globalization, redesigning our economy, influencing the way we live and play* p. 3: cyberjaya2.txt—3:6 (16:18)
	Teknologi Maklumat atau Information Technology (IT) adalah peneraju revolusi ini. *Information Technology (IT) is the spearhead of this revolution* p. 3: cyberjaya2.txt—3:45 (19:21)
	It has become clear to me that, as we all approach the 21st century, fantastic changes are taking place which make what was impossible in the old economy of the Industrial Age suddenly possible in the new world of the Information Age. p. 8: UcapanCyberjaya7.txt—8:4 (22:26)

	It was only a few years ago that we were so engrossed with the manufacturing industry and, hardly have fully extended it when we find ourselves in the information age. p. 9: UcapanCyberjaya8.txt—9:3 (22:25)
	Before our very eyes, the typewriter has become obsolete, the fax machine will eventually face the same fate and e-mail, which used to be an astonishing fascination only just six years ago, has now become as common as posting a letter. p. 9: UcapanCyberjaya8.txt—9:4 (27:31)
	As you can see Malaysia is preparing itself for the Information Age p. 9: UcapanCyberjaya8.txt—9:18 (216:217)
	In Malaysia, we are working hard to create the best environment to fulfill the promise of the Digital Age. p.12: UcapanCyberjaya11.txt—12:14 (136:137)
	Three main elements have brought mankind to the threshold of the Information Age—rapid advances in global communications, the Internet and convergence of technologies. p.13: UcapanCyberjaya12.txt—13:3 (17:20)
	Needless to say, Information Technology, which is the foundation of the new digital economy, is moving literally with the speed of light. p.13: UcapanCyberjaya12.txt—13:7 (46:48)
	Malaysia's IT Agenda defines the content of the mould as the creation of a Civil Society. p. 20: UcapanCyberjaya18.txt—20:20 (57:58)

	Thus in the MSC we are promoting the creative and risk-taking culture where knowledge workers can network and innovate in an environment which is most attractive for such activities. Cyberjaya is meant to be just this utopia and with the completion of its infrastructure in July last year, we are well on the way to creating such an environment. The MSC's excellent physical infrastructure will enable companies not only to deploy the latest technologies, but also develop new cutting-edge technologies. p. 2: UcapanCyberjaya20.txt—22:17 (84:93)

Theme: Economic Nationalism

In Table 24 below, I highlight examples of salient quotes that illustrate the idea of economic nationalism as professed by the leadership,

Table 24: Economic Nationalism

Economic Nationalism	Malaysians by and large know that the MSC represents their future and thus support and participation in this venture has permeated the whole society. p. 2: UcapanCyberjaya1.txt—2:11 (83:86)
	Kita juga mahu menjadi pengeluar barangan yang kita sendiri reka. *We want to also become a producer of the things we create.* p. 3: cyberjaya2.txt—3:24 (103:104)
	In Malaysia, we have taken a pragmatic approach to enter the Information Age. We realised that an I.T. Agenda is the sine qua non to realise our goal of becoming a fully developed nation by the year 2020. p.13: UcapanCyberjaya12.txt—13:9 (56:60)

	As we witness the death throes of the industrial era ethos and sense the birth of another—one that will be founded upon information and knowledge—should we not take it upon ourselves to manage our destinies instead of leaving it entirely to the free market system? p. 20: UcapanCyberjaya18.txt—20:3 (253:257)
	We want to generate high value—added economic activities covering all sectors of the economy and compete globally. While we compete globally, we also advocate co-operation and the sharing of experiences. The MSC is seen as our venture into the Information Age as well as the bridge to network among nations. p. 22: UcapanCyberjaya20.txt—22:6 (31:37)

Theme: Counter-hegemony

In Table 25 below, I present the examples of claims made that illustrate the idea of counter-hegemony.

Table 25: Counter-hegemony

Counter-hegemony	Walaupun Negara adalah komited dan menyokong konsep pasaran bebas dan globalisasi, namun Kerajaan tidak akan membiarkan konsep ini disalahgunakan oleh pihak yang tidak bertanggungjawab untuk merosak dan menghancurkan ekonomi negara kita. *Eventhough our Nation is committed to and support the concept of free enterprise and globalization, this Government cannot allow this concept to be abused by those who are irresponsible and those who will destroy our nation's economy* p. 14: UcapanCyberjaya13.txt—14:13 (122:127)

	KLIA adalah milik rakyat Malaysia dan kitalah yang akan menggunakannya lebih daripada orang lain. Gunakanlah KLIA dengan sebaik-baiknya. Tegurlah jika ada apa-apa yang tidak kena dan kita akan cuba memperbaikinya bersama. *KLIA [Kuala Lumpur International Airport] belongs to the people of Malaysia and it is us who will use it more than anyone else. Therefore, use it wisely. Give comments that will help us improve.* p. 18: UcapanCyberjaya17.txt—18:27 (319:322)
	Therefore, the move from Kuala Lumpur to Putrajaya is more than a physical migration. It is also symbolic of discarding old legacies and old mindsets—a move towards information—driven frameworks for performance-based management and services. And, we hope, this move will set in motion a paradigm shift in ways of thinking, working and living. p. 20: UcapanCyberjaya18.txt—20:45 (160:166)
	Kerajaan Tuanku tidak akan menghiraukan tuduhan—tuduhan ini kerana ia bukan sahaja tidak benar tetapi dibuat oleh orang yang lebih bersalah dalam perkara—perkara ini. Mereka tidak demokratik dengan tidak memberi hak kepada rakyat asli mereka dalam bidang politik, tidak membayar gantirugi selepas merampas harta orang asli, tidak mengendah suara ramai dalam forum antarabangsa, mencabul undang-undang negara asing dengan menculik warganegara untuk dibicara di bawah undang-undang mereka. Polis mereka memukul penunjuk perasaan, merantaikan kaki tangan banduan, memasang alatan di badan banduan yang boleh memberi kejutan eletrik dengan kemungkinan jantung banduan berhenti. Polis mereka menembak mati tanpa usul periksa dan mahkamah mereka mendapati polis tidak bersalah. p. 21: UcapanCyberjaya19.txt—21:19 (99:113)

Hegemony and Counter-hegemony

What are the dimensions of hegemony that has emerged from this study on Malaysia's Cyberjaya? I discern below, some initial ones. What follows will be a more elaborate discussion on the six levels of hegemony that emerge:

1. Perceptions of hegemony can be traced at the level of the state as an entity. In the case of Malaysia, the leadership of the Mahathir regime perceives that the "West" and its technological capability have been hegemonic at the level of global affairs. The "West" here means primarily the developed nations of the United States and Europe. Japan as a developed nation is looked upon as a role model of "Asian/Eastern superiority"

2. Developing nations develop strategies of technological progress as a means to counter-hegemonize the advanced industrial West. In the case of Malaysia, the use of Informational and Communicational Technologies, particularly the technology of the Internet as a national strategy (McClintock, 2001) of development is a means towards counter-hegemonizing. Hence, it is a response to the globalization process that is perceived by Malaysia to be hegemonized by the "West."

3. Developing states are aware of the power of advanced communications technologies as a means towards "capitalist mode" of progress and a way to be well integrated into the global capitalist system. This awareness is a "counter-hegemonizing" condition in itself.

4. At the level of the state, hegemony operates at the political leadership level, in response to question of globalization. The decision to create a grand real estate project such as Malaysia's Multimedia Super Corridor with its economic nucleus Cyberjaya is marketed to the Malaysia people as a national project and a nationalistic one too. The idea of nationalism is a hegemonic one too; large-scale projects that cost billions of Malaysia Ringgit are rationalized as projects that would benefit the *rakyat* or the common people.

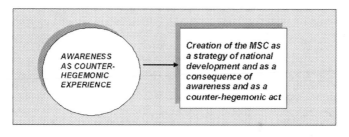

Figure 35: Consequence of Hegemony

Levels of hegemony

I will now discuss the five levels of hegemony derived from the findings in this study namely.

1. Philosophical
2. International economic/world systems
3. Regional
4. National ideological/base-super-structural
5. Familial/"the family success factor"
6. Psychological/popular cultural

Figure 36 below presents the complex inter-relationship between the levels of hegemony that operates at the different levels. Hegemony (of cybernetics) has its geneaology at the level of philosophy, rooted in language. The adoption and interpretation of the concept of cybernetics becomes a paradigm of economic progress that permeates thinking at the level of world-systems. The idea of informational capitalism as a feature of globalization and as a hypermodernized template of development becomes appealing to nations undergoing social and economic transformations. Nations, wanting to be known as "emerging markets" in the jargon of globalization theorists, adopt the developmentalist agenda that is governed by the philosophy of cybernetics or "technological determinism, or the idea that technology is a life-force in itself. When a nation embraces cyberneticism as philosophy of development, it alters its way of producing the means of subsistence of its people. Technology then changes the means of social relations and production and thereby creates a new form of consciousness; the technological consciousness. The new commanding heights of the new economy is "digital" in nature; that what installations to produce multimedia is now needed. In the case of Malaysia, the installation is the Multimedia Super Corridor which houses Cyberjaya, Putrajaya, The Multimedia University, and the Petronas Twin Towers.

Technology defines consciousness and newer mode of intellectual production is needed to meet the needs of the subsistence economy of the world's largest multinational corporations such as Microsoft, Lucent, and AOL-Time Warner as well as the Rupert Murdoch Dynasty. Because the newer consciousness need a newer definition of worker, the "knowledge worker" skilled in producing "multimedia products" are now needed. A successful worker must then be schooled successfully in the school buildings that will house multimedia production facilities guided by a cybernetic philosophy of education. At the level of the family, a child's success is defined as academic success; one that is based on credentialism whose standards are derived from the demands of the cybernetic industry. And finally, at the individual and psychological level, the mind is conditioned by the forces derived at the multitude of complex levels of hegemony of cyberneticism. The mind is influenced not only by the new tools the culture is using by most importantly by the houses that the minds inhabit.

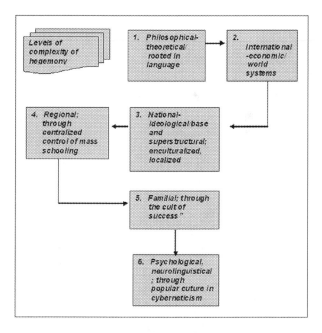

Figure 36: Complexity of Hegemony

In Figure 37 below, I present the character of hegemony as derived from this study.

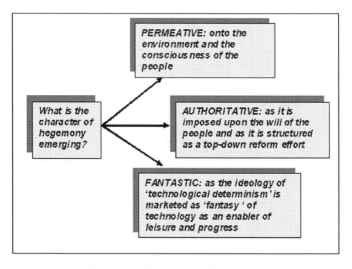

Figure 37: Character of Hegemony

Theme: Model of Success

Table 26: Model of Success

Model of Success	Knowledge that is accumulated from the outside is shared widely within the organisation, stored as part of the company's knowledge base, and utilised by those engaged in developing new technologies and products. A conversion process takes place where the knowledge from outside is converted and goes out again in the form of new products, services or systems. According to them, it is the effectiveness of this conversion process that fuels continuous innovation within Japanese companies, which in turn leads to competitive advantage. p. 5: UcapanCyberjaya4.txt—5:38 (170:180)
	This week, we have enjoyed an overwhelmingly positive response from the entertainment companies in Southern California and the high technology companies we saw at Stanford. p. 8: UcapanCyberjaya7.txt—8:3 (12:15)
	Even when Malaysia develops itself into a centre of educational excellence our engineers and managers still need to acquaint themselves with Japanese management and work ethics under the Look East policy. p. 10: UcapanCyberjaya9.txt—10:32 (182:186)
	The MSC is not just a physical location, or just another industrial or technology park—and it is not a Far Eastern imitation of the Silicon Valley—it represents a new paradigm in the creation of value for the Information Age. p. 13: UcapanCyberjaya12.txt—13:14 (81:85)

	The Cavendish Laboratory at Cambridge is just such an assembly of scientific intelligences. It has produced some of the world's greatest physicists. p. 13: UcapanCyberjaya12.txt—13:16 (228:231)
	Industri keluli memerlukan pelaburan yang besar yang tidak semestinya menjanjikan pulangan keuntungan dalam masa yang singkat. Pengalaman—pengalaman industri keluli di Amerika Syarikat, Jepun dan Korea Selatan menunjukkan mereka melalui proses yang sama dengan keuntungan hanya diperolehi selepas lama beroperasi. p. 15: UcapanCyberjaya14.txt—15:3 (29:35)
	Kita mahu menjadi sebuah negara perindustrian sepenuhnya menjelang 2020, di mana kita setanding dan setaraf atau lebih baik lagi daripada negara-negara yang telah lama mencapai status negara maju. p.15: UcapanCyberjaya14.txt—15:4 (37:40)
	We have the advantage of planning and working on a green field site, taking the best ideas from Japan, United States and even Germany to incorporate in this massive project. p.16: UcapanCyberjaya15.txt—16:13 (61:64)
	Through the Malaysia Incorporated Concept, we successfully transitioned from an agricultural-based economy to an industrial one within two decades. p. 20: UcapanCyberjaya18.txt—20:50 (181:184)

> The concept has been based on the experience of Silicon Valley and Route 128, the growth of ICT and the dynamism generated from the convergence of computing, telecommunications and content. We have not replicated the growth models of these hubs but we have innovated and advanced further on the basis of our interaction with the industries and the MSC's International Advisory Panel members. p. 22: UcapanCyberjaya20.txt—22:3 (17:25)

The figure below (Figure 38) represents a summary of the major sources of economic modeling as appropriated historically by the political administration that created the MSC. The advanced capitalist nations that have inspired Malaysia's economic growth are Great Britain, Japan, and The United States of America. The "inter-textuality" of the Malaysian economic system is derived from the sources outside of the nation and hence the forms of assistance and mentorship are derived from these major "texts".

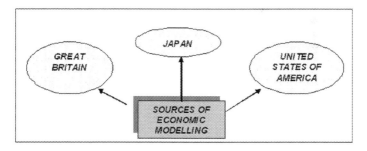

Figure 38: An inter-textualized Malaysian economics

Theme: Utopianism of a Networked Society

In Table 27 below, I present the salient quotes that illustrate the proclamation of the nature of utopia that is created.

Table 27: Utopianism of a Networked Society

Utopianism	to help create the vibrant, creative, networked society here in Cyberjaya. p. 2: UcapanCyberjaya1.txt—2:12 (74:76)
	Visinya lebih tinggi merangkumi konsep hubungan yang lebih bermakna antara petugas-petugas dalam Kerajaan, Kerajaan dengan rakyat dan Kerajaan dengan masyarakat perniagaan. p. 4: cyberjaya3.txt—4:15 (199:202)
	Third, the MSC will leapfrog available information infrastructures with a 2.5—10 gigabit Open Multimedia Network. This will use the latest ATM switches to provide Fiber to the Building. This network will have a 5 gigabit international gateway with direct links to Japan, North America, Europe, and other ASEAN countries. This will be operational by 1998. p. 6: UcapanCyberjaya5.txt—6:17 (103:109)
	Among others, our I.T. Agenda outlines various strategies which will help us achieve a knowledge society through the development of people, infrastructure and applications. p.13: UcapanCyberjaya12.txt—13:12 (71:74)

	we will install a high-capacity global telecommunications and logistics infrastructure built on the MSC's 2.5-gigabit to 10-gigabit digital optical fibre backbone and using the latest ATM switches to provide fibre to the building. This network will have a 5-gigabit international gateway with direct links to the U.S., Europe and Japan, as well as the other nations in South East Asia. p. 17: UcapanCyberjaya16.txt—17:38 (234:241)
	When the first phase is operational in January 1998, the new Kuala Lumpur International Airport will have 80 gates with two parallel runways. It will also become an integrated logistic hub with the latest technology and equipment to facilitate movements of people and goods. Cyberjaya is a city which will provide the physical and psychological environment for the pursuit of information age technologies and business. This city of intelligent buildings, multimedia enterprise estates, multimedia university, commercial and residential housing and recreation facilities will be able to support a living population of 100,000 people and a working population of 150,000 people. Putrajaya will be the new administrative centre of the Government. p.17: UcapanCyberjaya16.txt—17:42 (205:218)
	Malaysia's IT Agenda defines the content of the mould as the creation of a Civil Society. p. 20: UcapanCyberjaya18.txt—20:20 (57:58)

General Levels of Hegemony

Table 28: Levels of Hegemony

Philosophical level	in which the scientism of cybernetics, in the form of 'technological determinism' operates at the basic level of influence. In this study, the dominant theme for the rationale of developing The Multimedia Super Corridor and the two cities, Cyberjaya and Putrajaya is that of technological determinism. Technological progress is seen as inevitable, its march onwards to the drumbeat of informational capitalism. Philosophy, in this sense is driven by cyberneticism. At the counter-hegemonic level, Malaysia's state guiding philosophy spelled out the ethical and religious imperative in the development of human beings citizened by this state
International/ World Systems	in which the dominant hegemonic force is multinational corporatism primarily those that originate from advanced industrialized state of the so-called G-7 Nations. The composition of the Multimedia Super Corridor's International Advisory Panel attest to the idea that international hegemonic forces at work. At the counter-hegemonic level, Malaysia's nationalistic economic strategy utilizes the emerging high-speed informational and communicational technologies to create a "utopia" characterized by its hybrid of nationalism and cyberneticism,

Regional level	in which Southeast Asian states have resorted to the Idea that in order to be regionally competitive, national development must be enhanced through the use of tools of cybernetics. Thus in Malaysia as a unit of analysis, we saw the emergence of "technopoles" in Singapore, Taiwan, Hong Kong, and Japan, that are guided by the idea of regional competitiveness. Such is the nature of the hegemony of the philosophy of cybernetics that had driven national strategies in this region characterized by strong and authoritarian governance.
National-ideological	In which the ideological apparatuses of the strong state of Malaysia, are utilized in concert with informational technologies to not only strengthen the here and now economy and the utopia, but also to push the agenda for such social transformation with a virtually non-existent critical sensibility regarding the belief that technology is "value-neutral" and devoid of "political actors". At this level, dissent is silenced, in order for the rhetoric of developmentalism to prevail. At the counter-hegemonic level, nonetheless, informational and communication technology is used by dissenting voices to rapidize oppositionary movements. Malaysia's Bill of Guarantees states that it is the government's commitment to ensure that there will be no censorship of the Internet.
Familial level	in which there is a an emerging sense of families wanting their children to excel in the skills of computing as a result of the ideology of schooling that is in full operation. In Malaysia, the idea of success lies in the idea of success in schools that will translate into the idea of success in economic lives. The Malaysian Smart School movement is one which hegemonizes the nation into believing that the only way forward for the state is through the pathway of informational and communication technologies

Psychological level	n which the individual interaction with the computer, networked and linked globally, represents a personal hegemonic moment with the philosophy of cyberneticism and informational capitalism. At this level, the notion of neurolinguistic dimension of hegemony operates in which the human mind communicates with the world of cyberspace. In the case study of Malaysia, the hegemony of the English-language dominated Internet and the discourses embedded in the content and context will operate. The human-machine interaction will be the feature of the dialogical moments. The counter-hegemonic dimension of the national context of this interaction will be as such: the individual will be empowered to use communicate with others to subvert the state. The growth of websites critical to the ruling government illustrates the counter-hegemonic dimension of the application of cyberneticism.

General Themes Concerning "Utopianism"

I discern, from my findings, themes related to "utopia" and "dystopia." Figure 39 below illustrates the contradictions:

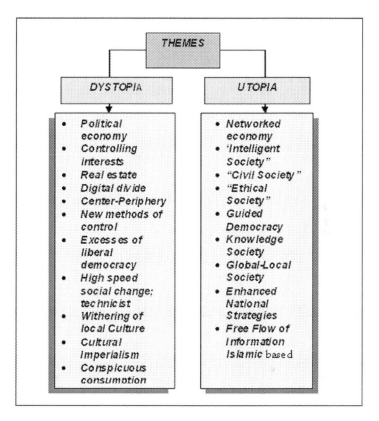

Figure 39: Cultural Contradictions of Cybernetic Capitalism

On the Contextual Flow of Hegemony

I refer to Figure 40 below on the flow of hegemony. Ideology is influenced by technological determinism and cybernetics, giving rise to hegemonic forces from outside. The developing nation-state appropriate the ideology of developmentalism to counter-hegemonize. The Gramscian notion of "hegemony" means the achievement of conformity and acceptance based on common sense because there is political, moral, and intellectual leadership defining the meaning of civil society. This is the classic meaning of the Gramscian concept, derived under the circumstances of Fordist thinking during the early stages of industrialization. However, in the case of post-industrialism, a variant of the definition of hegemony can be derived which explain the structure of cybernating nations.

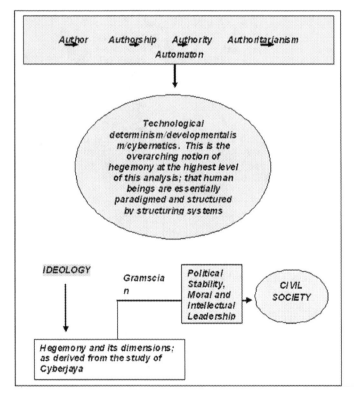

Figure 40: Contextual Flow of Hegemony

On the Dimension of Utopianism

This study yields an important finding on the dimension of utopianism. It is an Islamic utopianism blended with the model of Western capitalistic expansion. This is the "base" aspect of development of the nation-state if we look at the within the perspective of Marxist perspective of base and superstructure. Malaysia's history guides the will to create this new form of utopianism. These are the variations; a new image of Islam and national development, a new society with a strong religious (Islamic) foundation, a republic different from the ideology of Constitutional Monarchy, a corporation nation-state and a manufacturing hub of a globalized economy, a built environment to facilitate the development and nurturance of 'the technological consciousness', a marketplace to test ideas, and a real estate project whose beneficiaries might be those who are close to the national ruling party.

These are the variations of the dimensions of utopianism as it moves from the idea of a perfect society "a centrally-governed polis", "a cybernetic republic of techno-Malaya" to a real estate project with lesser utopian value but primarily motivated by huge profits from the construction of new territories that are based on expensive and extensive investment in high technology. Such is the fate of utopias, by way of a preliminary analysis. The figure below (Figure 41) summarizes the idea of the Malaysian utopia:

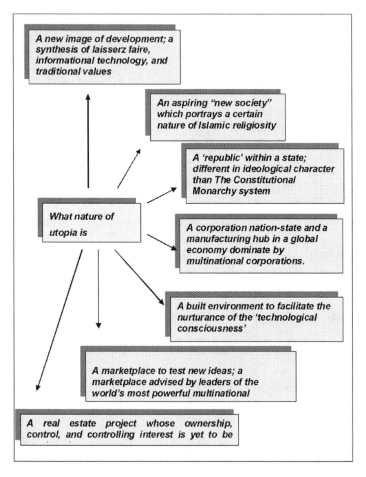

Figure 41: Nature of Utopianism

Conclusion

In the introductory section, I proposed to answer the following questions in this study of the nature of hegemony and utopianism; If we are to speak of hegemony, what might be its subdivisions? What will be its trans-cultural dimensions? If we are to explain a nation's utopian ideals what are its properties? The findings of this study conducted using mixed-method approach, suggested the nature of hegemony as operating from a multidimensional perspective (from philosophical/philological to the neuropsychological levels) and that the Malaysian utopia is a synthesis of hypermodernity and Islam.

Chapter XII

DISCUSSIONS ON GENERAL STATEMENTS CONCERNING LANGUAGE

"Culture has more to do with the houses we inhabit that with
the habits we acquire"

— Herve Varenne

Introduction

In the previous chapter I concluded with the idea
that hegemony is structured into the consciousness
of the nation through a strategy of disciplining and
controlling that arise out of the establishing of institutions
of control that are now inscribed onto the landscape
using informational communicational technologies. The
regime of the fourth prime minister Mahathir Mohamad
established institutions that uses advanced technologies to
enrich national strategies on the one hand, and to maintain
control beyond better than the imposition of raw power.
Hegemony permeates at various levels: philosophical to

psychological; structured by the institutions built and the ideological state apparatuses employed.

In my analysis of the genealogy of cybernetics I discover the transcultural flow of idea of technological determinism that has branched out into various levels of structurations and appropriated by the author to be embedded, as suggested by a philosopher of technology, into an inert form of nationalistic developmental policy (McClintock, 2001) that is wired up to the most advanced capitalist centers of the world. In the following sections I will discuss the implications of my findings and how they generate propositions and tools of analysis. I will first discuss some general statements concerning language particularly on the notion of the "intertextualized nation", and next discuss propositions concerning "cybernating nations" such as Malaysia, and finally discuss a set of tools I propose for the analysis of concepts that have genealogy and manifestations.

The "intertextualized" nation

The findings on Malaysia's grand project of social transformation can be looked at not only from the point of view of the flow of idea from one realm to another i.e from the realm of cybernetics to the physical-material realm of Cyberjaya but from a linguistic perspective as well. The digital text is inscribed onto a landscape; a process that fragments the soul of the nation and creates a hypermodern state that is authored and signatured by what is defined as "world-class companies". The "inter-textualized nation" is a consequence of Malaysia's developmentalist project of hypermodernity. The state becomes a neatly written subtext to a larger and more established matrix of Grand

Narrative called corporate capitalist developmentalism whose ideology and sophisticated tools of empire-ing is the forte of advanced industrial nations. Malaysia becomes a periphery wanting to be part of the Center, a subtext continually being written to tell the story of the text.

Kristeva (1980) writes about intertextuality as a linguistic situation in which one idea in a text is linked to another. The Self, in Kristeva's analysis is influenced by "subtexts" outside of itself that defines its textuality and as a consequence, loses its authenticity. A similar argument about the loss of authenticity is made by many a philosopher who writes about the consequence of modernity (Taylor, 1991) In this dissertation, the Malaysian MSC is an example of a nation that is ideologically linked to other ideas outside of the nation itself. In this case Malaysia's development is intertextualized with the idea of Western corporate interest by way of the advisory panelship, transfer of technology, and most importantly the colonization of corporate English Language onto the material and psychological development of the nation. The textuality of the nation is then characterized by the weaving of corporate and foreign discourses onto the developmentalist agenda of the nation, facilitating the withering of the nation-state and enhancing the role of the nation as a hypermodern Periphery of the Central capitalist nation of an equally hyper-modernized international capitalist system.

The "nation as text" becomes one that is continuously being co-authored by international inscribers interested in capitalizing on the cheap labor offered. The international inscribers were given the best of privileges such as generous ten-year tax-breaks, freedom from being harassed by worker unions since only "in-house unions" are allowed to exist, and state-of-the-art facilities to attract them to invest in the new Malaysian economy. The will to be "nationalistic" exists only in the form of signs and symbols that are touristic in nature, such as in the images and symbols of culture that are at the consumptive level and are merely showcases of tradition. The evidence gathered on the textuality of this nation lies in the signs and symbols in the cultural and industrial complexes; signs and symbols of predominantly American corporate business interests. Hence, not only the nation is inter-textualized by its linkages to other forces of influence, such as of the iconoclasms of Stanford University Area, United States of America, but also these signs and symbols are transmutating and hybridizing with the local hosts, as evident in the practice of street-naming on the campus of Malaysia's Multimedia University. In this sense, the development of the state parallels the development of the United States with regard to the influence of industries and corporations and the installations of technologies to march capitalism to its triumph (Noble, 1977; Noble 1984; Nye, 1990).

In the area of social reproduction, the schooling system, from the primary to tertiary levels, is turning towards the re-using of English Language as the language of Science and Technology and inscribed into the policy-making documents of languages of instruction. The emphasis of on the use of computer technology in schools, embalmed in the policy of creating Smart Schools to produce computer-literate workforce ("wired schools") parallels also the influence of computer giants in determining the nature of policy inscriptions on American public schools (National Commission on Excellence in Education, NCEEE, 1985) Such is an analysis of the intertextuality of Cyberjaya.

In the section below, I discuss propositions concerning the development of nations undergoing transformation such as Malaysia's.

Thirteen Propositions Concerning "Cybernating" Nations

From the findings of this study, I was able to generate propositions concerning nations undergoing transformations as a result of the utilization of newest informational communications technologies. Malaysia is an example of such as nation. The MSC is specifically its test-bed and Cyberjaya is an embodiment of a city built out of the regime's interpretation of the concept of cybernetics.

Table 29: Summary of Propositions on Cybernating Nations

ON CENTER-PERIPHERY THESIS	1. In a globalized post-industrialist world, the development of a cybernating nation will continue to follow, to a degree or another the Center-Periphery pattern of development.
ON COMPLEXITY SYSTEMS	2. Pure historical materialist conception of change cannot fully explain why nations cybernate; the more a nation gets "wired" the more complex the interplay between nationalism and internationalism will be.

ON SEMANTIC/ STRUCTURALISM	3. The more a nation transforms itself cybernetically, the more extensive the enculturalization and transformation of the word "cybernetics" will be.
ON THE POLITICAL-ECONOMY OF LINGUISTIC TRANSFORMATION	4. The extent of the enculturalization of the concept of "cybernetics" will determine the speed by which a nation will be fully integrated into the global production-house of the telematics industry
ON AUTHORITARIANISM	5. The stronger the authority of the regime the greater the control and magnitude of the cybernating process. In a cybernating nation, authority can reside in the political will of a single individual or in a strong political entity, consequently producing the author's "regime of truth".
ON THE WITHERING OF THE NATION-STATE	6. The advent of the Internet in a developing nation signifies the genesis of the erosion of the power of government-controlled print media. Universal access to the Internet will determine the total erosion of government-produced print media. Subaltern voices will replace Grand Narratives.

ON CENTER-PERIPHERY AND GLOBALIZATION THEORY	7. Creative consciousness of the peoples of the cybernating nation will be centralized in the area of business and the arts, modeled after successful global corporations.
ON RESISTENCE	8. Critical consciousness of the people of the cybernating nation will be centralized in the area of political mobilization and personal freedom of expression, modeled after successful Internet-based political mobilization groups.
ON HEGEMONY/ CENTER-PERIPHERYTHESIS	9. At the macro-level of the development of a nation-state, the contestation of power is between the nation cybernating versus the nations fully cybernated, whereas at the micro level, power is contested between the contending political parties/groups.
ON RESISTENCE	10. The more the government suppresses voices of political dissent, the more the Internet is used to affect political transformations
ON MODERN IMPERIALISM	11. The fundamental character of a nation will be significantly altered with the institutionalization of the Internet as a tool of cybernating change. The source of change will however be ideologically governed by external influences, which will ultimately threaten the sovereignty of the nation-state

ON DEEP-STRUCTURING	12. Discourse of change, as evident in the phenomena of cybernation, is embedded in language. The more a foreign concept is introduced, adopted, assimilated, and enculturalized, the more the nation will lose its indigenous character built via schooling and other means of citizenship enculturalization process
ON PARADIGM OF RESEARCH	13. Postmodernist perspectives of social change (discourse theory, semiotics, Chaos/Complexity theory) rather than those of Structural-Functionalists, Marxist, or neo-Marxist, can best explain the structure and consequences of cybernetic changes.

These thirteen propositions most obviously need to be refined in order for us to look at the phenomena of transcultural consequence of computer-mediated communications from perspectives beyond ones that may be characterized by pure Structural—Functionalists or neo-Marxists.

Formulations concerning "Tool of Transcultural Analysis"

From data analyses on the various nature of "inscriptions" and from the propositions generated, we move on to our findings concerning the idea of "transcultural flow of ideas" I suggest we use as a method to analyze concepts that are enculturalized. There are 13 components to the idea and the discussions will be part of looking at the possibility of going beyond theory generating but to develop a set of tools for cultural analysis especially as it pertains to the *problematique* of cultural imperialism and hegemony of concepts.

Drawing from some of the findings in this analysis and in thinking of the term hegemony in the analysis of the transcultural and transmutational flow of the concept "cybernetics", I'd like to propose how we look at ideas and conjure a paradigm of looking at how they become hegemonizing. I use the word "culture" in transcultural flow to refer to the idea of "a culture of cybernetic capitalism" that has come to color the developmentalist agenda of many a developing nation. I use to the word "transmutate" to refer to the process of synthesis an hybridization of, at the most macro of all levels, the cultures that come into contact with each other and, at the most micro of levels, the words that come into existence by an arranged marriage in the hypermodern developmentalist scheme of things. The words in Figure 39 below represent my own understanding of how we may arrive at a systematic analysis of foreign words by looking at the dimensions of the case:

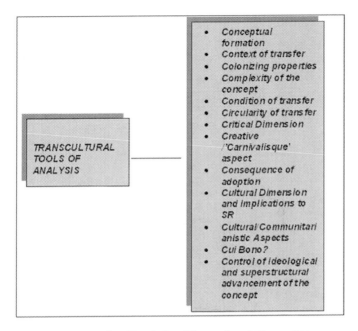

Figure 42: Tools of Analysis of Transcultural Flow of Ideas

Transcultural Tools of Analysis as Process of Subjectivizing

The findings of this study has allowed me to present a table of explanation on how hegemonic formulations can be analyzed. The idea of cybernetics as it progresses from its philological roots in the idea of the explanation into the behavior of living systems onward to its evolution as a systems theory to its appropriated and hybridized version in the case of Malaysia' Cyberjaya and the MSC, is an example of an idea that can be analyzed as a transcultural process. I analyzed Cyberjaya and the MSC as a genealogy. In the table below (Table 30) I present the parts of the tool for analyzing hegemonic ideas that have history and consequences. I call the strategy "tool of analysis for trans-cultural flow of ideas "to highlight the idea of ideological migration from one cultural system to another and to analyze it as a phenomena of social change that has its roots and consequences in the social relations of production.

Table 30: Tools of Analysis of Transcultural Flow of Ideas

1. CONCEPTUAL FORMATION	How did the idea begin? (i.e. history, philology, genealogy). What is its genesis? What are its historical materialistic dimensions?
2. CONTEXT OF TRANSFER	Was the concept imposed upon the people? How did it get transplanted—through colonization? Neo-colonization? Did it evolved naturally out of the cultural tradition of the people? (One may look at the impact of the Iranian Revolution on the Islamic world.)
3. COLONIZING PROPERTIES	How hegemonic is it?, due to it foreignness, Do we need the people to possess a high level of technical knowledge to understand and apply the concept.
4. COMPLEXITY OF THE CONCEPT	Is the idea still difficult to be understood? Does the society need a restructuring in the architecture of knowledge in order to understand the concept as its subdivisions?
5. CONDITION OF TRANSFER	What is the nature of the social history of the recipient nation/people? How has the people tried itself to understand the new concept? How has the ideological state apparatus played a historical role in developing the base-superstructural foundation of hegemony?

6. CIRCULARITY OF TRANSFER	How has the concept evolved from a point of origin and gets enculturalized). One may look at examples from the media and visual arts.
7. CRITICAL DIMENSION OF THE CONCEPT	What are the contradictions inherent in the concept?
8. CREATIVE DIMENSION	What is so appealing and novel about the concept. What are the liberal and illiberal democratic dimensions of the concept?
9. CONSEQUENCE OF ADOPTION	What are the changes that happened when the concept was adopted and becomes a network of enterprise of policies? How were people, geography, places, and technology affected?
10. CULTURAL DIMENSION AND IMPLICATION	What is the nature of the relationship of the new concept to the social relations of production?
11. CULTURAL/COM UNITARIANISTIC ASPECT	Is the concept democratic? If so, is it of the nature liberal or illiberal? Is it of the nature protectionist, participatory, or pastoral democracy?
12. CUI BONO or 'WHO BENEFITS'?	Who/what institutions benefit from the institutionalization of the concept? What form of class structure did it create? What contradiction did it bring
13. CONTROL of IDEOLOGICAL AND SUPER-STRUCTURAL ADVANCEMENT	How is the concept advanced/ ideology of it pushed or marketed? What institutional and political support is given to the idea (see for example the Islamization of management in Malaysia)

The above represent my ideas and analyses on what might be developed as tools of cultural analysis in looking at transcultural flow of ideas. These tools are indeed a series of questions to inquire into the kaleidoscopic nature of a concept, such as the inquiry into the transformation of "cybernetics" to "Cyberjaya" which illustrated a range of issues the tools of analysis as above can be utilized. In other words, tools here means to deconstruct and to get to the genealogy and the maturity of the concept itself. Because these series of questions attempt to provide foundations to the 'dialecticness" of the concept in question an further inquire into the 'materialistic' foundation of the concept, these tools can be looked at as 'counter-foundational' it is a philosophical and dialogical enterprise.

Hegemony does not exist in a vacuum, nor transplanted onto the landscape of peoples. Concepts become hegemonic after a series of transformations aided by fertile ground of such growth. The fertility might be in the form of political stability, authoritarianism in the way the national leadership advances such formations, or simply via clever marketing of the concept itself. Herein lies the need to perform a surgical-cultural analysis of the genealogy of the conceptual transformations.

I believe we may now need to arrive at a Theory of Hegemonic Formations if we can find relationships between the dependent and independent variables to concepts discussed in the context of transcultural flow of ideas. This dissertation on hegemonic formations, from the concept of cybernetics to the conditions of the creation of Cyberjaya, can perhaps be a good illustration of this theory. Concepts such as 'jihad', 'democracy', 'peacekeeping', 'globalization', 'freedom', can be put to such analysis by the tools I propose.

Implications for further inquiry

To elaborate, below are some of the illustrations of the applicability of this concept of transcultural flow of ideas as it further relates to the study of Malaysia:

- Constitutional monarchy
- Nationalism
- Parliamentary democracy
- Liberal Education
- Islamic Education
- Islamization
- Islamic Reformation

In answering the question of the process of "cybernation" and how cultures change and new social conditions emerge, and how we are to look at phenomena from a kaleidoscopic perspective, I propose thenceforth, any concept be analyzed from the above thirteen lenses of conceptual formulation.

I hope that through this study, we may then design more studies on states undergoing a conscious counter-hegemonizing process. Furthermore we can discern the creative dimensions of the strategies used by different nations and finally formulate models to further inquire into the structure of "cybernetic" revolutions (see Kuhn, 1996).[16] In other words, we can embark upon in-depth and longitudinal studies of the ways in which

---

[16] Historian of Science, Thomas Kuhn's classic proposition is that scientific revolutions are the phenomena of breaking out of the thresholds of discoveries when older scientific belief systems "crumble." Kuhn gave an example of the Copernican

nations control or are being controlled specifically by "digital communication technologies," how social relations are reorganized, and how these states are integrated into the continuing complexities of the global capitalist system.

Revolution and its impact on the idea of the "terresterialization of man."

Chapter XIII

POSTSCRIPT: ON HEGEMONY, TECHNOLOGY, AND AUTHORITY

"Man, in a word, has no nature; what he has is—history . . .
what nature is to things, history . . . is to man."

—Ortega y Gassett

Introduction

The production of this dissertation began with a conceptualization of an explanation of the process of how hegemony operates at the subtlest of all levels: language and the practice of everyday lives. It describes the creation of new spaces of power constructed from the ideological archives of the old and those that domesticate the dominated, to borrow Bourdieu's term (1984). Using semiotics as one of the triangulated tool of analyses, the process of hegemonic formation is explained. In other words, the means and methods of inscribing the ideology of cyberneticism is described. The newly-created cities of Cyberjaya and Putrajaya in the hypermodernized developmentalism of Malaysia are examples of how the global telematics conglomerate of the advanced capitalist world, particularly of the United States of America and Japan are invited exclusively to inscribe their brand of practices and signature economies onto a willing state such as Malaysia. Such an inscriptural enterprise is made possible by the "coalition of the willing" of the political and economic decision-makers of this state. The English language in general and that of American corporatism in particular becomes the instrument by which the inscriptions onto the landscape of ideology and infrastructure are made.

The MSC after Mahathir

Mahathir Mohamad, the creator of the MSC and the iron hand that sculptured the landscape which is now another form of an engine of growth, left a legacy of developmentalism that continues to define the style of his successor Abdullah Ahmad Badawi. The MSC continues to flourish as a real estate venture and a business area.

Mahathir Mohamad survived his 22-year rule, exited gracefully, and continue to be honored by different states, institutions, as well as his own, UMNO (United Malays National Organization), party members. He was and will continue to be awarded honorary doctoral degrees from several local institutions and conferred the highest title in the country, "Tun". The honoring of Mahathir also symbolizes the honoring of the technocratic leadership he nurtured.

The way the nation is governed, vis-à-vis hegemony, technology, and authority is reflected not only in the purpose of the creation of the MSC but in the way the nation is governed. Counter-hegemonic policies and pronouncements at international and national forums continue to be made in the post-Mahathir era.

Hegemony, Technology and Authority

In the previous chapters I conclude my finding on the nature of hegemony and utopianism in the case of Malaysia's MSC as further exemplified in the case of the creation of the city of Cyberjaya. The idea of installations creating ideology and expression is central to my early proposition. I began with the premise that signs and symbols determine the nature and character of hegemony. How hegemony is structured is a complex, yet recognizable process. Hegemony alone does not merely sustain ideology. This notion is perhaps applicable to the case of hegemonic formations in societies that is controlled by corporate-controlled media but not in authoritarian states in transitional societies elsewhere such as Malaysia. Authority defines the character and furtherance of hegemony as well as the facilitation of hegemonic transitions.

Cybernetic technology is such a technology, in this study, employed as a structuring tool by state authority that lies in one person who ruled for a considerable period of time. The authoritarianism in the Malay culture itself, appropriated by the authoritarianism of the modern Malay political leadership, aided by the authoritarianism inert in technology perceived as deterministic creates newer social systems, better systems of control, and more efficient systems of irrigation for global capitalism. The development of consciousness is dependent upon the development of literacy; in the case of Cyberjaya and the

MSC, the language of cybernetics hegemonizes over the language of the agrarian society that is tied in to the peoples of the land and to to that of natives. In the 22 year—reign of Mahathir Mohamad, the state saw a transformation of such a language, of cybernetics, appropriated and translated into social action and transforming the social relations of production to create "non-reproductive" forces of society such as national institutions and communication systems, besides the creation of "productive" forces such the means of "multimedia" production whose ends justify their links to the global capitalist economy. Hence, hegemony works in harmony with authority to create a hegemonic condition to further advance, in this case the cause of the transnational capitalistic struggle to dominate the world economy.

Whilst many a philosopher and historian of technology such as McClintock (1992) see the potentials of the technology of the Internet in for example, in democratizing society and intellectualizing the individual through education, in many a society such as Malaysia the technologizing of the polity itself becomes a natural process of creating a culture that not only is forced to be structured into the mould of a consumerist and international capitalistic economy but one that will be disabled (McDermott & Varenne, 1995) by the very technology perceived to be democratizing.

I end this study on hegemony and utopianism in a Southeast Asian state; with a renewed affirmation of Marx's thesis on technology, culture, and the development of consciousness.

References

Abdulla, R. (2000). *Words of paradise: Selected poems of Rumi.* New York, NY: Penguin Studio.

Abrams, M. H. (1971): *The Mirror and the lamp: Romantic theory and the critical tradition.* London: Oxford University Press.

Adorno, T. (1991). Freudian theory and the pattern of fascist propaganda. In J.M. Bernstein (Ed.), *The culture industry: Selected essays on mass culture.* London: Routledge.

Adshead, R. (1989). *Mahathir of Malaysia: Statesman and leader.* London: Hibiscus

Ahmad, K. (1966). *Characterization in Hikayat Hang Tuah: A general survey of methods of character portrayal and analysis and interpretation of the characters of Hang Tuah and Hang Jebat.* Kuala Lumpur: Dewan Bahasa dan Pustaka.

Alatas, S. H. (1977). *The myth of the lazy native:* London: Frank Cass.

Andaya, B.W., & Andaya, L.Y. (1982). *A history of Malaysia.* London:The Macmillan Press.

Anderson, B. (1991) *Imagined communities. Reflections on the origin and spread of nationalism* (Rev. ed.). New York: Verso.

Ang, I. (1985). Dallas and the ideology of mass culture. In S. During (Ed.), *The cultural studies reader.* London: Routledge.

Appadurai, A. (1996). Disjuncture and difference in the global cultural economy. In A. Appadurai (Ed.), *Modernity at large.* Minneapolis: University of Minnesota Press.

Armstrong, K. (1993). *Muhammad: A biography of the Prophet.* San Francisco, CA: Harper Collins.

Ashton, D., & Greene, F. (1996). *Education, training, and the global economy._*Brookfield, VT: Edmund Elgar Publishing Company.

Bagdikian, H. H. (1983). *Media monopoly.* Boston, MA: Beacon Press.

Bakunin, M. (1953). Idealism and materialism. In G. P. Maximoff (Ed.), *The political philosophy of Bakunin: Scientific anarchism.* London: Collier-Macmillan.

Barnet, R., & Muller, R. E. (1974). *Global reach: The power of the multinational corporations.* New York: Simon and Schuster.

Bastin, J., & Winks, R. W. (Eds.). (1979). Malaysia. Selected historical readings (2nd. ed.). Netherlands: KTO Press.

Bauman, Z. (1998) *Globalization. The human consequences.* New York, NY: Columbia University Press.

Bell, D. (1973). *The coming of the post-industrial society.* New York: Basic Books.

Bell, D. (1976). *The cultural contradictions of capitalism* (20th Anniversary ed.). New York: Basic Books.

Bellah, R. N., Madsen, R., Sullivan, W. M., Swidler, A., & Tipton, S. M. (1985). Habits of the heart. Individualism and commitment in American life. Berkeley, CA: University of California Press.

Beniger, J. R. (1986). *The control revolution. Technological and economic origins of the information society.* Cambridge, MA: Harvard University Press.

Bennett, B. T., & Robinson, C. E. (Eds.) (1990). *The Mary Shelley Reader: Containing Frankenstein, Mathilda, tales and stories, essays and reviews, and letters.* New York: Oxford University Press.

Bertalanffy, L. V. (1968). General Systems Theory—A critical review. In W. Buckley (Ed.), *Modern systems research: Overview.* Chicago, IL: Aldine.

Bourdieu, P. (1994). Structures, habitus, power: Basis for a theory of symbolic power. In N. B. Dirks, G. Eley, & S. B. Ortner (Eds.), *Culture/Power/History*. Princeton, NJ: Princeton University Press.

Bradell, R. (1980). *The study of ancient times in the Malay peninsula and Straits of Malacca*. Kuala Lumpur: The Malaysian Branch of the Royal Asiatic Society.

Bredo, E., & Feinberg, W. (1982). *Knowledge and values in social and educational research*. Philadelphia, PA: Temple University Press.

Buber, M. (1958). *I and Thou* (2nd ed.) (R. G. Smith, Trans.). New York: Collier Books.

Buck, W. (1978). *Ramayana* retold. Ontario: New American Library.

Buckley, C. B. (1984). *An anecdotal history of old times in Singapore 1819-1867*. Singapore: Oxford University Press.

California Newsreels (1978). *Controlling interest: The World of the Multinational Corporations*, sound filmstrip.

Camus, A. (1975). The myth of Sisyphus. In W. Kaufmann (Ed. & Trans.), *Existentialism. From Dostoevsky to Sartre*. New York, NY: Meridian Book.

Carnoy, M., & Levin, H. (1985). *Schooling and work in the democratic state.* Stanford, CA: Stanford University Press.

Castells, M. (2000). *The rise of the network society* (2nd ed., Vol. 1). Malden, MA: Blackwell Publishers.

Castells, M., & Hall, P. (1994), *Technopoles of the world. The making of 21st century industrial complexes.* New York: Routledge.

Central Intelligence Agency (CIA). (2003). *CIA factbook.* Retrieved July 5, 2003, from http://www.cia.gov/cia/publications/factbook/geos/my.html.

Cheah, B. K. (1999). Politics. Malaysian political development from colonial rule to Mahathir. In A. Kaur, & I. Metcalfe (Eds.), *The shaping of Malaysia.* London: Macmillan Press.

Chin, A. (1994). *The communist party of Malaya. The inside story.* Kuala Lumpur:Vinpress.

Chomsky, N. (1989). *Necessary illusions. Thought control in democratic societies.* Boston, MA: South End Press.

Chomsky, N. (2001). *9-11.* New York: Seven Stories Press.

Claeys, G., & Sargent, L. T. (Eds.) (1999). *The utopia reader.* New York: New York University Press.

Cleary, T. (Trans.) (1993). *The essential Koran. The heart of Islam. An introductory selection of readings from the Qur'an.* New York, NY: Harper San Francisco.

Coedès, G., & Damais, L. (1992). The Kota Kapur inscription. *Sriwijaya. History, religion, & language of an early Malay polity* (Monograph no. 20). Kuala Lumpur: Malaysian Branch Royal Asiatic Studies.

Connery, S., Hertzberg, M., & Tollefson, R. (Producers). (2000). *Entrapment.* Twentieth Century Fox.

Csikszentmihalyi, M. (1996). *Creativity: Flow and the psychology of discovery and invention.* New York: Harper Perennial.

de Certeau, M. (1984). *The practice of everyday life* (S. Rendall, Trans.). London: University of California Press.

Denzin, N. K., & Lincoln, Y. S. (Eds.). (1994). *Handbook of qualitative research.* Thousand Oaks, CA: Sage Publications.

Descartes, R. (1996). Meditations on first philosophy in L. E. Cahoone (Ed.), *From modernism to postmodernism: An anthology.* Malden, MA: Blackwell Publishers. (Reprinted from Meditations on first philosophy. (E. Haldane & G. R. T. Ross, Trans.) in *The philosophical work of Descartes,* Vol. 1, pp. 144-157, 1975, Cambridge: Cambridge University Press). (Original work published 1641)

Dewey, J. (1997). *Experience and Education.* New York: Simon and Schuster

Eagleton, T. (1991). *Ideology. An introduction*. New York: Verso.

Eco, U. (1976). *A Theory of Semiotics*. Bloomington, IN: Indiana University Press.

Ellul, J. (1964) *The technological society*. New York: Vintage Books.

Ellul, J. (2003). Extracts from 'autonomy' (J. Neugroschel, Trans.). The 'autonomy' of the technological phenomena. In R. C. Scharff & V. Dusek, (Eds.). *Philosophy of technology. The technological condition. An anthology* (pp. 386-397). Oxford: Blackwell Publishing. (Reprinted from *The technological system*, pp. 125-150, 335-338, 1980, New York: Continuum Publishing)

Esslin, M. (2001). *Theatre of the absurd*. London: Methuen Press.

Fairclough, N. (1992). *Discourse and social change*. Malden, MA: Blackwell Publishers.

Fallows, J. (2003). The Age of Murdoch. *The Atlantic Online* (2003, September). Retrieved November 6, 2003, from http://www.theatlantic.com/ issues/2003/09/ fallows.htm

Fanon, F. (1967). *Black skin, white masks* (C. L. Markmann, Trans.). New York: Grove Press.

Foley, D. (1984). Colonialism and schooling in the Philippines, 1898-1970. In P. G. Altbach & G. P. Kelley. (Eds.), Education and the colonial experience. New Brunswick, NJ: Transaction.

Foucault. M. (1978). Discipline and punish. The birth of the prison (A. Sheridan, Trans.). New York: Pantheon.

Frank, A. G. (1966). The development of underdevelopment. *Monthly Review, 18* (4), 17-31.

Frank, A.G. & Gills, B.K. (Eds.) (1993). *The world system. Five hundred years or five thousand?* New York, NY: Routledge.

Freire, P. (1986). *Pedagogy of the oppressed.* New York: Continuum.

Friedmann, J. (1992). *Empowerment. The politics of alternative development.* Cambridge, MA: Blackwell Publishers.

Friedman, M. (1982). *Capitalism and freedom.* Chicago: University of Chicago Press.

Funston, J. (1980). *Malay politics in Malaysia. A study of UMNO and party Islam.* Kuala Lumpur: Heinemann Educational Books.

Funston, J. (2001). Malaysia. Developmental state challenged. In J. Funston (Ed.), *Government and politics in Southeast Asia.* New York, NY: Zed Books.

Geertz, C. (1971, Winter). Deep play: Notes on the Balinese cockfight. *Daedalus*, 1-38.

Geuss, R. (1981). *The Idea of a Critical Theory: Habermas and the Frankfurt School*. London: Cambridge University Press.

Gitlin, T. (1983). *Inside prime time*. New York: Pantheon Books.

Glaser, B. G., & Strauss, A. L. (1967). *The discovery of grounded theory: Strategies for qualitative research*. New York: Aldine de Gruyter.

Gleick, J. (1988). *Chaos. Making a new science*. New York: Viking Press.

Gomez, E. T., & Sundram, J. K. (1999). *Malaysia's political economy: Patronage and profits* (2nd ed). Cambridge: Cambridge University Press.

Gramsci, A. (1971). Americanism and fordism. In Q. Hoare & G. N. Smith (Eds. & Trans.), Selections from the prison notebooks of Antonio Gramsci. (pp. 277-318). New York: International Publishers.

Gramsci, A. (1992). Hegemony and separation of powers. *Prison notebooks. European perspective series*. New York, NY: Columbia University Press.

Gross, B., & Gross, R. (Eds.) (1985). *The great school debate*. New York: Simon and Schuster.

Gruber, H. (1993). Creativity in the moral domain: Ought implies can implies create in *Creativity Research Journal 6* (1 & 2). New Jersey: Ablex Publishing Corporation.

Gruber, H. E. (1989). The evolving systems approach to creative work. In D. B. Wallace & H. E. Gruber, (Eds.), *Creative people at work. Twelve cognitive case studies.* New York: Oxford University Press.

Gruber, H., & Wallace, D. (1978). The case study method and evolving systems approach for understanding unique creative people at work. In R. Sternberg (Ed.), *Handbook of creativity.* New York: Cambridge University Press.

Gullick, J. M. (2000). *A history of Kuala Lumpur 1856-1939.* Selangor: The Malaysian Branch of Royal Asiatic Society.

Habermas, J. (1971). *Knowledge and human interest.* Boston: Beacon Press.

Hall, S. (1993). Encoding, decoding. In S. During (Ed.), *The cultural studies reader.* London: Routledge.

Hardt, M., & Negri, A. (2000). *Empire.* Cambridge, MA: Harvard University Press.

Harrington, M. (1977). Twilight of capitalism. New York: Simon and Schuster.

Heidegger, M. (2003). The question concerning technology. In R. C. Scharff & V. Dusek, (Eds.), *Philosophy of technology: The technological condition. An anthology* (pp. 252-264). Oxford: Blackwell Publishing. (Reprinted from *Basic writings* (Rev. ed.)., pp. 311-314, 1993, New York: HarperCollins)

Heussler, R. (1981). *British rule in Malaya. The Malayan civil service and its predecessors, 1867-1942.* Westport, CT: Greenwood Press.

Hilley. J. (2001). *Mahathirism, Hegemony and the new opposition.* New York: Zed Books.

Horkheimer, M. (1973). *Eclipse of reason.* New York: Continuum.

Ivanov, V.V. (1977). The role of semiotics in the cybernetic study of man and collective. In D. P. Lucid (Ed. & Trans.), *Soviet Semiotics: An anthology.* Baltimore, MD: The John Hopkins University Press.

Jacq-Hergoualc'h, M. (2002). *The Malay peninsula. Crossroads of the maritime silk road (100 B.C. – 1300 A.D.).* Leiden: Brill.

Jameson, F. (1988). *The ideologies of theory. Essays 1971-1986* (Vol. 2). Minnesota: University of Minnesota Press.

Jameson, F. (1991). *Postmodernism, or, the cultural logic of late capitalism.* Durham, NC: Duke University Press.

Jay, M. (1973). *The dialectical imagination.* Boston, MA: Little, Brown, and Company.

Jefferson, T. (2003). Representatives of the United States of America. In B. Blaisdell, *The communist manifesto and other revolutionary writings. Marx, Marat, Paine, Mao, Ghandi, and others* (pp. 63-66). Mineola, NY: Dover Publications. (Reprinted from J. Grafton (Ed.) (2000), *The declaration of independence and other great documents of American history, 1775-1864*, Mineola, NY: Dover Publications. Original work published 1776)

Kargon, R. H., & Molella, A. P. (2000). Culture, technology and constructed memory in Disney's new town: Techno-nostalgia in historical perspective. In M. R. Levin (Ed.), *Cultures of control.* Amsterdam: Harwood Academic Publishers.

Kauffmann, W. (Ed. & Trans.). (1975). *Existentialism from Dostoevsky to Sartre.* New York, NY: Meridian Book.

Kegan, R. (1982), *The evolving self: Problem and process in human development.* Cambridge, MA: Harvard University Press.

Kellner, D. (1989). *Critical theory, Marxism and modernity.* Baltimore, MD: The Johns Hopkins University Press.

Kershaw, R. (2001). Monarchy in Southeast Asia: The faces of tradition. Politics in Asia series. New York: Routledge.

Khoo, B. T. (1995). Paradoxes of mahathirism: An intellectual biography of Mahathir Mohamad. Kuala Lumpur: Oxford University Press.

Khoo, K. K. (1991). *Malay society. Transformation & democratisation. A stimulating and discerning study on the evolution of Malay society.* Subang Jaya, Selangor: Pelanduk Publications.

Knorr-Cetina, K. D. (1983) The ethnographic study of scientific work: Towards a constructivist interpretation of Science. In K. D. Knorr-Cetina & M. Mulkay (Eds.), *Science Observed.* London: Sage Publications.

Kress, G., & van Leeuwen, T. (1996). *Reading images. The grammar of visual design.* New York: Routledge.

Kristeva, J. (1980). *Desire in language: A semiotic approach to literature and art.* New York, NY: Columbia University Press.

Kuhn, T. (1996). *The structures of scientific revolutions* (3rd ed.). Chicago, IL: University of Chicago Press.

Lefebvre, H. (1996). *Writings on cities* (E. Kofman & E. Lebas, Trans.). Malden, MA: Blackwell Publishers.

Lekomcev, J. K. (1977). Foundations of general semiotics. In D. P. Lucid (Ed. & Trans.), *Soviet Semiotics: An anthology.* Baltimore, MD: The John Hopkins University Press.

Lenin, V.I. (1916). Imperialism the highest stage of capitalism, a popular outline. Retrieved November 6, 2003, from http://www.fordham.edu/halsall/mod/1916/Lenin-imperialism.html

Lincoln, Y. S., & Denzin, N.K. (1998). The fifth moment. In N. K. Denzin & Y. S. Lincoln, (Eds.), *The landscape of qualitative research: Theories and issues.* Thousand Oaks, CA: Sage Publications.

Maaruf, S. (1984). *The concept of a hero in Malay society.* Singapore: Eastern University Press.

Manuel, F.E., & Manuel, F. P. (1979). *Utopian thought in the western world.* Cambridge, MA: Harvard University Press.

Marcuse, H. (1941). Some social implications of modern technology. *Studies in Philosophy and Social Sciences,* (Vol. IX).

Marcuse, H. (1964). *One-dimensional man. Studies in the ideology of advanced industrial society.* Boston, MA: Beacon Press.

Marcuse, H. (1985) Some social implications of modern technology. In A. Arato & E. Gebhart (Eds.), *The essential Frankfurt School reader.* New York: Continuum.

Marx, K., & Engels, F. (1955). *The Communist Manifesto.* In Samuel H. Beer (Ed.) North Brook, IL: Att M Publishing Corporation.

Marx, K., & Engels, F. (1967). *The Communist manifesto* (S. Moore, Trans.). Middelsex, England: Pelican Books Ltd. (Original translated work published 1888)

Marx, L. (1964/2000). *The machine in the graden: Technology and the pastoral ideal in America.* New York: Oxford University Press.

Mason, A., & Silver, J. (Producers), & Wachowski, A., & Wachowski, L. (Directors). (1999). *The Matrix.* [Motion picture]. United States: Warner Brothers.

Matthews, J. H. (1974). *Theatre in dada and surrealism.* Syracuse, NY: Syracuse University Press.

Mauzy, D. K. (1983). *Barisan Nasional: Coalition government in Malaysia.* Kuala Lumpur: Maricans.

McClintock, R. (1992) *The Educators Manifesto: Renewing the Progressive Bond with Posterity through the Social Construction of Digital Learning Communities.* New York: Institute for Learning Technologies.

McClintock, R. (2001). Personal Conversation at a Dissertation Proposal Hearing session. Teachers College, Columbia University, New York City, New York.

McDermott, R., & Varenne, H. (1995) Culture *as* disability. *Anthropology and Education Quarterly 26*(3), 324–348.

McLaren, P. (1997). *Revolutionary multiculturalism: Pedagogies of dissent for the new millennium.* Boulder, CO: Westview Press.

McMichael, P. (1996). Development and social change. A global perspective. Thousand Oaks, CA: Pine Forge Press.

Memmi, (1965). The *colonizer and the colonized* (H. Greenfeld, Trans.). Boston, MA: Beacon Press. (Original translated work published 1957)

Milne, R. S., & Mauzy, D. K. (1986). *Malaysia: tradition, modernity, and Islam*. Boulder: Westview Press.

Milne, R. S., & Mauzy, D. K. (1999). *Malaysian politics under Mahathir*. London: Routledge.

Milner, A. C. (1982). *Kerajaan. Malay Political Culture on the eve of colonial rule*. Tucson, AZ: The University of Arizona Press.

Mitton, R. (1997). "Special report malaysia: The man behind the vision," in Asiaweek,
Retrieved, November 6, 2003, from
http://www.asiaweek.com/asiaweek/97/0509/cs1.html

Moggie, L. (2002). Communications. In high gear into the knowledge society. In M. Yeoh (Ed.), *21ˢᵗ century Malaysia. Challenges and strategies in attaining vision 2020*. London: Asean Academic Press.

Mohamad, M. (1970). *The malay dilemma*. Singapore: Times Books International.

Mohamad, M. (1986). *The challenge*. Kuala Lumpur: Pelanduk Publications.

Mohamad, M. (1991). *Malaysia: The way forward*. Paper presented at the inaugural meeting of the Malaysian

Business Council, 28 January. Retrieved February 25, 2003, from http://www.moe.gov.my/carta.htm

Mohamad, M. (1995). *The early years. 1947-1972.* Kuala Lumpur: Berita Publishing.

Mohamad, M. (1998). *Excerpts from the speeches of Mahathir Mohamad on the multimedia super corridor.* Subang Jaya, Selangor: Pelanduk Publications.

Mohamad, M. (2002). Education. Sowing the seeds of great minds. In M. Yeoh (Ed.), *21ˢᵗ century Malaysia. Challenges and strategies in attaining vision 2020.* London: Asean Academic Press.

More, T. (1999). Utopia. In G. Claeys & L. T. Sargent (Eds.), *The utopia reader.* New York: New York University Press. (Original work published 1516)

Morrison, A. (1997). ed. "I am still here: Asiaweek's complete interview with mahathir mohamad". Retrieved November 7, 2003, from http://www.asiaweek.com/asiaweek/97/0509/cs2.html

Muhr, T. (1997). *Atlas ti* (Version 4.2). [Computer Software]. Thousand Oaks, CA: Scolari.

Multimedia Development Corporation [MDC]. (n.d.). *Cyberjaya: The model intelligent city in the making.* Kuala Lumpur: Author.

Multimedia Development Corporation [MDC]. (1997). *Unlocking the potential of the information age.* Kuala Lumpur: Author.

Multimedia Development Corporation [MDC]. (2003). *About the Multimedia Super Corridor.* Retrieved July 28, 2003, from http://www.msc.com.my/msc/msc.asp.

Multimedia Development Corporation Corporate Affairs Department [MDC CAD]. (n.d.). *Malaysia in the new millennium.* Kuala Lumpur: Author.

Mumford, L. (1966). *The myth of the machine. Technics and human development.* New York: Harcourt, Brace & World.

Naisbitt, J. (1984). *Megatrends.* New York: Warner Books.

Nasr, S. H. (1964). *An introduction to Islamic cosmological doctrines: Conceptions of nature and methods used for its study by the Ikhwan al-Safa, al-Buruni, and Ibn Sina.* Cambridge, MA: Harvard University Press.

National Commission on Excellence in Education [NCEE] (1985). A nation at risk. In B. Gross & R. Gross (Eds.), *The great school debate.* NY: Simon and Schuster.

Negroponte, N. (1995). *Being digital.* New York: Alfred A. Knopf.

Neske, G., & Kettering, E. (1990). Martin Heidegger and national socialism. Questions and answers (L. Harries Trans.). New York: Paragon House.

Noble, D. F. (1977) *America by design. Science, technology, and the rise of corporate capitalism.* New York: Oxford University Press.

Noble, D. F. (1984). *Forces of production: A social history of industrial automation.* New York: Alfred A. Knopf.

Nye, D. (1990) Electrifying America: Social meanings of a new technology, 1880-1940, Boston, MA: MIT Press.

Ochse, R. (1990). *Before the gates of excellence: The determinants of creative genius.* New York: Cambridge University Press.

Ongkili, J. P. (1985). *Nation-building in Malaysia 1946-1974.* New York: Oxford University Press.

Orwell, G. (1948). *Nineteen eighty-four.* London: Secker and Warburg.

Osman, M. T. (Ed.). (1997). *Islamic civilization in the Malay world.* Kuala Lumpur: Dewan Bahasa dan Pustaka.

Papert, S. A. (1999). *Mindstorms: Children, computers, and powerful ideas.* New York: Basic Books.

Parenti, M. (1993). Inventing reality. The politics of the mass media. New York: St. Martin's Press.

Pathmanathan, M. (1990). *Malaysia and world affairs: The mahathir impact.*
Petaling Jaya: Economic Research Associates.

Pelli, C. (2003). *Petronas Towers.* Retrieved November 16, 2003, from
http://www.cesar-pelli.com/flash.cfm

Plato (1961). Phaedo (H. Tredennick, Trans.). In E. Hamilton & H. Cairns (Eds.), *The collected dialogues of Plato including the letters.* Princeton, NJ: Princeton University Press. (Reprinted from *The last days of Socrates* (H. Tredennick, Trans.), 1954, Harmonsworth, Middlesex: Penguin Classics)

Plato (1993). *Republic. Plato* (R. Waterfield, Trans.). NY: Barnes & Noble Books.

Plato (2003). On dialectic and "techne". In R. C. Scharff & V. Dusek, (Eds.), *Philosophy of technology: The technological condition. An anthology* (pp. 8-18). Oxford: Blackwell Publishing. (Reprinted from *Republic VII* (G. M. A. Grube & C. D. C. Reeve, Trans.) pp. 186-206, 210-212. 1992, Indianapolis: Hackett)

Postman, N. (1993) *Technopoly. The surrender of culture to technology.* New York: Vintage Books.

Putrajaya Holdings. (1997). *Putrajaya: The federal government administrative centre.* Kuala Lumpur: Author.

Radhakrishnan, S., & Moore, C. A. (Eds.). (1957) *A sourcebook in Indian philosophy*. Princeton, NJ: Princeton University Press.

Rahner, K. (1985). *Foundations of Christian faith: An introduction to the idea of Christianity* (W.V. Dyck, Trans.). New York: Crossroads.

Reinecke, I. (1984). *Electronic illusions. A skeptic's view of our high-tech future* (Rev. ed.). USA: Viking Penguin.

Renan, E. (1990). What is a nation? (M. Thom, Trans.). In H. K. Bhabha (Ed.), *Nation and narration*. New York: Routledge.

Rendra, W. S. (1979). *The struggle of the Naga tribe (Kisah perjuangan suku Naga)* (M. Lane, Trans. & Intr.). New York: St. Martin's Press.

Richard J., Barnet R. J., & Muller, R. E. (1974) *Global reach: The power of the multinational corporations*. New York: Touchstone.

Ritzer, G. (1998). *The Mcdonalization thesis.* London: Sage Publications.

Rose, G. (2001). *Visual methodologies.* Thousand Oaks, CA: Sage Publications.

Rosenblueth, A., Wiener, N., & Bigelow, J. (1968). Behavior, purpose, and teleology. In W. Buckley (Ed.), *Modern systems research.* Chicago, IL: Aldine.

Rostow, W. W. (1960). *The stages of economic growth. A non-communist manifesto.* Cambridge, MA: Cambridge University Press.

Rousseau, J. J. (1979). *Emile or On education* (A. Bloom, Trans.). New York: Basic Books.

Rousseau, J. J. (1987). *On the social contract.* (D.A. Cress, Trans.& Ed.). Indianapolis, IN: Hackett Publishing Press.

Rousseau, J. J. (1992). *Discourse on the origin of inequality* (D. A. Cress, Trans.). Indianapolis, IN: Hackett Publishing Company. (Original work published 1755)

Said, E. (1993). *Culture and imperialism.* New York: Vintage Books.

Said, E. W. (1978). *Orientalism.* New York: Vintage Books.

Said, M. I., & Emby, Z. (Eds.). (1996). *Malaysia: Critical perspectives. Essays in honor of Syed Husin Ali.* Petaling Jaya: Persatuan Sains Sosial Malaysia.

Salleh, M. H. (1999). *Menyeberangi sejarah: Kumpulan esei pilihan.* Kuala Lumpur: Dewan Bahasa dan Pustaka.

Sartre, J. P. (1975) Existentialism is a humanism. In W. Kaufmann (Ed. & Trans.), *Existentialism. From Dostoevsky to Sartre.* New York, NY: Meridian Book.

Saussure, F. d. (1983): *Course in general linguistics* (R. Harris, Trans.). London: Duckworth. Original work published 1916)

Schimmel, A. (1985). *Mystical dimensions of Islam.* Chapel Hill, NC: University of North Carolina Press.

Schmidt, W. H., & Finnigan, J. P. (1993). *TQM Manager: A practical guide for managing in a total quality organization.* San Francisco, CA: Josey Bass Publishers.

Schultz, T. (1971). *Investment in human capital.* New York: The Free Press.

Seers, D. (1972). What are we trying to measure? *The Journal of Development Studies, 8,* 21-26.

Shellabear, W. G. (Ed.) (1964). *Hikayat seri rama.* Singapore: Malaysia Publishing House.

Simon, H. (1977, March 18). The social impact of computers: What computer mean to Man and Society. *Science,* 195.

Simon, H. A. (1996). *The Sciences of the artificial* (3rd ed.). Cambridge, MA: The MIT Press.

Smith, A., & Hutchinson, J. (Eds.). (1995). *Nationalism.* Oxford: Oxford University Press.

Spielvogel, J. J. (2003). *World History. Modern Times.* New York, NY: Glencoe McGraw-Hill.

Steiner-Khamsi, G. (2000). Transferring education, displacing reforms. In J. Schriewer (Ed.), *Discourse formation in comparative education*. New York: Peter Lang.

Stockwell, A. J. (Ed.). (1995). *British documents on the end of empire. Malaya. Part III. The alliance route to independence 1953-1957*. London: HMSO.

Strauss, A., & Corbin, J. (1998) *Basics of qualitative research: Techniques and procedures for developing grounded theory* (2nd ed.). Thousand Oaks, CA: Sage Publications.

Syed-Omar, S. M. (1993). *Myths and the Malay ruling class*. Singapore: Times Academic Press.

Tarling, N. (2001). *Imperialism in Southeast asia. 'A fleeting, passing phase.'* New York, NY: Routledge.

Taylor, C. (1991). *The ethics of authenticity*. Cambridge, MA: Harvard University Press.

Teeuw, A. (1979). *Modern Indonesian Literature II*, 2 Vols., The Hague: Martinus Nijhoff.

Thurow, L. (1997). Plate two: An era of man-made brainpower industries. In *The future of capitalism*. New York: Penguin Books.

Toer, P. A. (1993). *Child of all nations* (M. Lane, Trans.). New York: William Morrow.

Toffler, A. (1970). *Future Shock*. New York: Bantam Books.

Turkle, S. (1997). *Life on the screen. Identity in the age of the internet.* New York, NY: Touchstone.

Van Leeuwen,T., & Jewitt, C. (Eds.) (2001). *Handbook of visual analysis.* Thousand Oaks, CA: SAGE Publications.

Varenne, H. (n.d). Retrieved August 28, 2003, from, http://www.users.globalnet.uk/~fhs/idealpalace.htm

Varenne, H. (2002) Retrieved November 6, 2003, from, http://varenne.tc.columbia.edu/class/tf5003.html

Varenne, H. (2003). Constraints, possibilities, and the anthropological imagination. Retrieved November 15, 2003, from http://varenne.tc.columbia.edu/class/tf6514/tf6514.html

Vavrek, G. M. (1992). An American lead the Japanese and the U.S. follows. In P. F. Fendt & G. M. Vavrek (Eds.), *Quality improvement in continuing higher education and service organizations.* Wales: Edwin Mellen Press.

Wallace, D., & Gruber, H. (Eds). (1989) *Creative people at work: Twelve cognitive case studies.* New York: Oxford University Press.

Wallerstein, I. (1979). *The Capitalist world economy.* Cambridge: Cambridge University Press.

Wallerstein, I. (1981). Dependence in an interdependent world: The limited possibilities of transformation within the capitalist world economy. In H. Munoz (Ed.) *From dependency to development: Strategies to overcome underdevelopment and inequality*. Boulder, CO: Westview Press.

Wallerstein, I. (1990). Culture as the ideological battleground of the modern world-system. In M. Featherstone (Ed.), *Global culture, nationalism, globalism and modernity*. Newbury Park, CA: SAGE Publications.

Wiener, N. (1954). *Human use of human beings: Cybernatics and society*. New York: Da Capo Press.

Wignaraja, P. (1993). Rethinking development and democracy. In P. Wignaraja (Ed.), *New social movements in the South*. New Jersey: Zed Books.

Williams, R. (1977). *Marxism and literature*. New York: Oxford University Press.

Willlis, P. (1977) *Learning to Labor: How Working Class Kids Get Working Class Jobs*. New York: Columbia University Press.

Zinn, H. (1980). A people's history of the United States. New York: Harper and Row Publishers.

Appendix A

(Sample note on September 11, 2001)

Appendix B

Members of the Multimedia Super Corridor International Advisory Panel

Chairman:	Dato' Seri Dr Mahathir Mohamad, Prime Minister, Malaysia

Secretary:	Tan Sri Dato' Dr Othman Yeop Abdullah (Executive Chairman) Multimedia Development Corporation

Members:	Dr Stan Shih (Chairman & CEO) The Acer Group
	Mr Serge Tchuruk (Chairman & CEO) Alcatel Alsthom
	Dr Gilbert F. Amelio (Senior Partner) Sienna Ventures
	Mr. Jean C. Monty (Chairman of the Board) BCE Incorporated

Mr Michael R. Bloomberg (Founder & CEO)
Bloomberg L.P.

Mr. Ben Verwaayen (Chief Executive)
British Telecom

Prof. Shumpei Kumon (Executive Director)
Centre for Global Communications
International University of Japan

Ambassador Diana Lady Dougan (Chaiman)
Cyber Century Forum

Mr John P. Morgridge (Chairman of the Board)
Cisco Systems Inc.

Mr. Michael D. Capellas (President & CEO)
Compaq Computer Corporation

Mr. Charles B. Wang (Chaiman)
Computer Associates

Dr. Terry Cutler (Managing Director)
Cutler & Company

Mr. Uwe R. Doarken (Chairman & CEO)
DHL Worldwide Express

Mr. Don Tapscott
Digital 4Sight

YBhg Datuk Michael S. Dell (Chairman & CEO)
Dell Computer Corporation

Mr. Richard H.Brown (Chairman &
CEO)
EDS Corporation

Mr. Ragnar Back (Executive Vice
President & President)
Ericsson

Mr. Tadashi Sekizawa (Chairman)
Fujitsu Limited

Dr. Edwin J. Feulner (President)
The Heritage Foundation

Mr N.R. Narayana Murthy (Chairman of
the Board and Chief Mentor)
Infosys Technologies Limited

Mr Louis Gerstner Jr (Chairman of the
Board & CEO)
International Business Machines
Corporation (IBM)

Dato' Dr Craig R Barrett (President &
CEO)
Intel Corporation

Prof Wang Xuan (Director)
Institute of Computer Science &
Technology, Peking University

Mr. Bon-Moo Koo (Chairman)
LG Chemicals Inc. & LG Electronics

Mr Ben Verwaayen (Vice Chairman)
Lucent Technologies

Mr. Robert Madge (Chairman &
President, Madge Networks NV)
Madge Networks Ltd

Mr. Bill Gates (Chairman & Chief
Software Architect)
Microsoft Corporation

Mr Jack Valenti (President & CEO)
Motion Picture Association (MPAA)

Mr. Chris Galvin (Chairman of the Board
& CEO)
Motorola

Dato' Dr Tadahiro Sekimoto (Chaiman
Emeritus)
NEC Corporation

Mr. Jun-Ichiro Miyazu (President)
Nippon Telegraph & Telephone
Corporation

Mr Jorma Olilla (Chairman of the Board
& CEO)
Nokia Corporation

Dr. Kenichi Ohmae (Managing Director)
Ohmae & Associates

Prof. Derek Williams (Executive Vice
President)
Oracle Corporation

Mr Peter Job (CEO)
Reuters Group PLC

Ir. Anton Hendrik Schaaf (Member of the
Group Executive Board)
Siemens AG

Prof. Dr. Henning Kagermann (Co-
Chairman & CEO)
SAP AG

Mr. Robert Bishop (Chairman & CEO)
Silicon Graphics Inc.(SGI)

Mr. Masayoshi Son (President & CEO)
Softbank Corporation

Mr. Nobuyuki Idei (President & CEO)
Sony Corporation

Professor Michael Spence (Altholl
McBean Professor of Economics and
Dean Emeritus)
Stanford University, Graduate School of
Business

Professor William F. Miller (Herbert
Hoover Professor of Public and Private
Management Emeritus)
Stanford Graduate, School of Business

Dr. John Gage (Chief Researcher and
Director of Science Office)
Sun Microsystems Inc.

Mr. Jim Barksdale (Partner)
The Barksdale Group

Mr. Alvin Toffler (Founder)
Toffler & Associates

Mr. Philip A. Odeen (Executive Vice
President and General Manager)
TRW Systems & Information Technology
Group

Professor Sir Alec Broers (Vice ChancellorEmeritus Professor of Electrical Engineering)
Vice Chancellor's Office, University of Cambridge

Mr. Jim Manzi (Member of the Board of Directors)
Invicta Networks Inc

Appendix C

Complete themes and subthemes derived from the 21 Prime Ministerial speeches on Cyberjaya and the MSC

AWARENESS OF/ COUNTER-HEGEMONY	censorship as a serious problem economic shifts equity and access to ICT ethics of technological determinism global producer globalization and competition misuse of information need for high tech investment need for universal access paradox of ICT revolution potentials of ICT problems of decentralization problems of Info Age reaping economic benefits regional nationalism revolution for all uses and abuses of new technology

COUNTER HEGEMONY	competitive edge global participant regional leader counter hegemony creation of knowledge workers education global participant ICT as tool

GLOBALIZATION	global competition global economy: national participation global manufacturing global test-bed. globalization globalization: as collaboration globalization: competition globalization: multicultural synthesis globalization: technological determinism

HEGEMONY	advisory panel technological consciousness Center-Periphery Developmentalism

NATIONAL	MSC as national ICT strategy national advantage national agenda national agenda: initiative national agenda: resource mobilization national aspiration national confidence national development via ICT national economy: high speed growth national ICT strategy national labor-force national pride: Malaysians as good workers national pride: model of progress national pride: nation as producer national priority national strategy national strategy: global participant national strategy: guarantees national strategy: ICT

Technological determinism
Technological progress

UTOPIA (nature of,)	electronic village borderless world definition of knowledge worker eco-friendly environment electronic government ethos of a civil society human development and ICT ICT as enabler of civil society ICT investment haven ideological state apparatuses information-rich society knowledge and productivity knowledge society knowledge workers nationalism networked society ownership of knowledge participatory democracy re-creating the nation rule of the wise Stanford-inspired telecommunications network vision of world peace advanced nation status by year 2020 intelligent cities the republic of Cyberjaya for Malaysian people top-down reform social improvement via ICT

Appendix D

Speeches of the Prime Minister Cited and Analyzed

(Occasion/Title, Place, and Date)

THE INFOTECH MALAYSIA `96
MERDEKA HALL, PUTRA WORLD TRADE
CENTRE
December 12, 1996

THE OFFICIAL OPENING OF CYBERJAYA
CYBER VIEW LODGE
July 8th, 1999

MAJLIS PELANCARAN KEMPEN TEKNOLOGI
MAKLUMAT (IT)
AUDITORIUM BESAR, ANGKASAPURI, KUALA
LUMPUR
October 11th. 1997

MAJLIS ANUGERAH KUALITI PERDANA
MENTERI DAN SIMPOSIUM KEBANGSAAN
KERAJAAN ELEKTRONIK
PUSAT DAGANGAN DUNIA PUTRA, KUALA
LUMPUR
December 18th. 1997

THE OFFICIAL OPENING OF THE MULTIMEDIA
UNIVERSITY

THE MEETING WITH SILICON VALLEY CHIEF
EXECUTIVE OFFICERS OF HIGH
TECHNOLOGY COMPANIES
WESTIN HOTEL, SANTA CLARA, CALIFORNIA
January 17th. 1997

THE MALAYSIA—US BUSINESS COUNCIL
ROUNDTABLE AND INAUGURAL
MEETING
NEW YORK, USA
September 28th. 1999

THE LUNCHEON JOINTLY HOSTED BY SIX
JAPANESE ECONOMIC ORGANISATIONS
TOKYO, JAPAN
March 27th. 1997

MAJLIS PERASMIAN LITAR LUMBA SEPANG
SEPANG, SELANGOR
March 9th. 1999

DIGITAL ENTERTAINMENT IN THE
NETWORKED WORLD

BEVERLY HILLS HOTEL, LOS ANGELES
January 14ᵗʰ. 1997

THE MSC INVESTORS CONFERENCE IN
CONJUNCTION WITH CEBIT
HANNOVER, GERMANY
March 20ᵗʰ. 1998

ISTIADAT PERTABALAN SERI PADUKA
BAGINDA YANG DI-PERTUAN AGONG YANG
KE-11
ISTANA NEGARA, KUALA LUMPUR
September 23, 1999

PERASMIAN KILANG BEAM & SECTION
KEDAH DARUL AMAN
May 12ᵗʰ. 1997

THE OFFICIAL LAUNCH OF SIEMENS
FUTUREL@B (FUTURE LAB)
PETRONAS TWIN TOWERS, KLCC
July 6ᵗʰ. 1999

THE CHILEAN-MALAYSIAN BUSINESS
LUNCHEON
SANTIAGO, CHILE
September 29ᵗʰ. 1997

MAJLIS PERASMIAN LAPANGAN TERBANG
ANTARABANGSA KL
SEPANG, SELANGOR
Jun 27ᵗʰ. 1998

THE MULTIMEDIA ASIA 1997 (MMA `97)
CONFERENCE AND EXHIBITION
THE MINES RESORT CITY, SERI KEMBANGAN,
SELANGOR DARUL EHSAN
September 16th. 1997

MAJLIS MENGADAP DAN ISTIADAT
PENGURNIAAN DARJAH KEBESARAN
SEMPENA ULANGTAHUN HARI KEPUTERAAN
SERI PADUKA BAGINDA YANG DI-PERTUAN
AGONG ISTANA NEGARA, KUALA LUMPUR
Jun 3rd. 2000

MALAM 'ASIA PACIFIC MSC IT&T AWARDS'
(APMITTA)
HOTEL PALACE OF THE GOLDEN HORSES
March 31st. 2000